P9-EAJ-544

THE
10
Most Important
Things You
Can Say to a

MORMON

RON RHODES

HARVEST HOUSE PUBLISHERS
Eugene, Oregon 97402

Verses marked NIV are taken from the Holy Bible: New International Version®. NIV®. Copyright © 1973, 1978, 1984 by the International Bible Society. Used by permission of Zondervan Publishing House. The "NIV" and "New International Version" trademarks are registered in the United States Patent and Trademark Office by International Bible Society.

Verses marked NASB are taken from the New American Standard Bible ®, © 1960, 1962, 1963, 1968, 1971, 1972, 1973, 1975, 1977, 1995 by The Lockman Foundation. Used by permission.

Verses marked KJV are taken from the King James Version of the Bible.

Cover by Dugan Design Group, Bloomington, Minnesota

THE 10 MOST IMPORTANT THINGS YOU CAN SAY TO A MORMON
Copyright © 2001 by Ron Rhodes
Published by Harvest House Publishers
Eugene, Oregon 97402
www.harvesthousepublishers.com

Library of Congress Cataloging-in-Publication Data
  Rhodes, Ron.
    The 10 most important things you can say to a Mormon / Ron Rhodes
      p. cm.
    ISBN 978-0-7369-0534-3
    1. Mormon Church—Controversial literature.   2. Witness bearing (Christianity)   3. Apologetics. I. Title: Ten most important things you can say to a Mormon. II. Title. III. Series.

  BX8645.R47 2001
  289.3—dc21
                                                     2001024089

All rights reserved. No part of this publication may be reproduced, stored in a retrieval system, or transmitted in any form or by any means—electronic, mechanical, digital, photocopy, recording, or any other—except for brief quotations in printed reviews, without the prior permission of the publisher.

Printed in the United States of America

12   13   14   15   16 / BP-CF / 14   13   12   11   10

To the countless Christians across America who hold full-time jobs (often more than 40 hours per week), have families to take care of at home, and are very busy in life's various endeavors—yet still desire to defend the truth of Christianity against cultic intruders. May this little book assist you in reaching that worthy goal!

Acknowledgments

A special thanks to the staff at Harvest House Publishers for coming up with the idea for this concise treatment on Mormonism.

I also want to take this opportunity to thank the thousands of people who contacted me following the publication of my earlier book, *Reasoning from the Scriptures with the Mormons* (a considerably longer book available in Christian bookstores). Your words of encouragement and commitment to the cause of apologetics among cultists have been an inspiration to me.

Most of all, as always, I give a heartfelt thanks to my wife, Kerri, and our two children, David and Kylie, without whose support it would truly be impossible for me to do what I do.

Contents

Introduction

This book is short on purpose. The chapters are short on purpose. I believe there is something to be said for brevity. However, *brevity should not be thought of as shallow.* This book contains ten powerful points to share with your Mormon friends. You'll discover the most important apologetic information in the most concise and succinct method possible. In our day of information overload, the merits of this approach are obvious.

Each chapter makes one primary point, but also includes a number of supportive arguments that substantiate that particular point. My desire is that you not only have the necessary information to "hold your own" in confrontations with Mormons on the doorstep, but that you also become equipped to lead Mormons to the true God, the true Jesus, and the true gospel of grace presented in the New Testament. I pray that God will use you to bring Mormons out of the kingdom of darkness and into the kingdom of light—the kingdom of Jesus Christ (see Colossians 1:13).

If the information in this book causes you to want to go deeper and learn even more about interacting with Mormons, that is great. The more you learn, the more God can use you in witnessing. In such a case, I urge you to pick up and dig in to my larger volume, *Reasoning from the Scriptures with the Mormons* (432 pages, Harvest House Publishers, 1995). You will find that these two books complement each other nicely. In fact, for your convenience, at the end of each chapter I provide relevant page numbers from the larger book.

Icons Used in This Book

To make this informative guide easier to follow and understand, the following icons highlight specific sections.

 Mormon position on a particular doctrine.

 Key points summarized from the preceding text regarding the Mormon position.

 Biblical position on a particular doctrine.

 An important point when refuting Mormon theology or supporting biblical truth.

 A closer look at an important word, verse, or historical insight.

 Witnessing tip.

 Proceed with caution on a particular point.

 Quick review of apologetic points.

 Digging deeper—recommends supplementary reading from my book *Reasoning from the Scriptures with the Mormons*.

The Mormon Church
Is Not the "Restored Church"

One day in the spring of 1820, Joseph Smith was reading the Bible at James 1:5: "If any of you lacks wisdom, he should ask God, who gives generously to all without finding fault, and it will be given to him." That verse suddenly came alive to him. He determined to ask God which church to join, so he went into the woods to pray. He claims his question was answered in a vision in which he encountered two personages—the Father and the Son. Smith recounts how "the Son" instructed him not to join any of the churches, for they were all wrong: "The Personage who addressed me said that all their creeds were an abomination in his sight."[1]

The Church of Jesus Christ of Latter-day Saints (Mormons) teaches that total apostasy engulfed the church soon after the death of the last apostle; therefore the "one true church" needed to be restored. This apostasy is said to be prophesied in Scripture. For instance, Acts 20:30,31 says: "Even from your own number men will arise and distort the truth....So be on your guard!" (See also Acts 3:20,21; 2 Thessalonians 2:3.) Mormons claim that proper church organization, with its respective offices, was lost, along with continual revelation through God's appointed representatives. The true gospel was also lost in its completeness from the Bible due to "designing priests" removing its "plain and precious" truths (see Galatians 1:8). Further, the Aaronic and Melchizedek priesthoods disappeared after the death of the last apostle.

Joseph Smith allegedly restored proper church organization, the true gospel, and the "eternal" priesthood.[2] Mormons, citing Psalm 110:4 and Hebrews 5:6, believe the presence or absence of this priesthood (both Aaronic and Melchizedek) establishes the divinity or falsity of a professing church. Because the Mormon church *exclusively* has this "restored" priesthood, it alone is the one true church. All other churches of Christendom are said to be apostate.

 Key Points to Remember—Mormon Claims of a Restored Church

- Total apostasy overcame the church after the death of the last apostle.

- This apostasy involved the loss of proper church organization, the true gospel, new revelation from God's spokesmen, and the priesthood.

- The Mormon church is the restored church.

 What does the Bible say? Specifically, 1) *it does not* prophesy a total apostasy in the early church; 2) *it does not* contain promises of a restored church; 3) the priesthood belongs only to Christ, so the Mormon claim of restoring the Melchizedek priesthood is impossible. Furthermore, biblical and secular history disproves the claim that the Mormon church is the restored church. In recent years, the Mormon church has even downplayed its claim to exclusivism as the "restored" church.

 The Bible *does not* prophesy a total apostasy in the early church. Let us consider the two primary passages

Mormons cite in support of their view—Galatians 1:6-8 and 2 Thessalonians 2:3.[3]

Galatians 1:6-8

> I am astonished that you are so quickly deserting the one who called you by the grace of Christ and are turning to a different gospel—which is really no gospel at all. Evidently some people are throwing you into confusion and are trying to pervert the gospel of Christ. But even if we or an angel from heaven should preach a gospel other than the one we preached to you, let him be eternally condemned!

This passage records the apostle Paul's warning against believing a *different* gospel. Notice that there is no indication that there would be a *total* apostasy of the entire church throughout the world. The local church in Galatia was the focus of these statements by the apostle Paul.

The Galatians had apparently succumbed to a gospel that added works to faith. Certain Jewish Christians, unhappy with the way Paul freely invited Gentiles to come to God, had begun to visit the churches he had established. Their purpose was to "Judaize" these Gentile believers—to persuade them that after believing in Christ they needed to take the additional step of getting circumcised.[4] This effectively added "law" to the "grace" Paul had been preaching. Galatians 3:1,3 says, "You foolish Galatians!...After beginning with the Spirit, are you now trying to attain your goal by human effort?"

Paul responded by emphasizing that *any* gospel that contradicted the gospel of grace already authoritatively handed down to them is to be rejected. He even held himself accountable to this standard (see Galatians 1:8; 1 Corinthians 15:3).

A Counterfeit Gospel

The gospel of Mormonism is one of works, which contradicts the gospel of grace taught by Paul (Ephesians 2:8,9). The Mormon gospel falls into the category of "a different gospel" (Galatians 1:8).

2 Thessalonians 2:3

> Don't let anyone deceive you in any way, for that day will not come until the rebellion occurs and the man of lawlessness is revealed, the man doomed to destruction.

Mormons say this verse speaks of an apostasy that would engulf the entire church, making a restoration imperative.[5]

Contrary to the Mormon view, 2 Thessalonians 2:3 *does not* say there would be a total apostasy of the entire church. Paul was referring not to a general global apostasy but rather to a specific, distinguishable apostasy that is *still to come* (see 1 Timothy 4:1-3; 2 Timothy 3:1-5; 4:3,4; James 5:1-8; 2 Peter 2; 3:3-6; Jude).[6]

🔍 *Eisogesis* v. *Exegesis*

Eisogesis refers to reading a meaning into the text of Scripture. *Exegesis* refers to deriving a meaning from the text. Mormons often engage in eisogesis. Their interpretation of 2 Thessalonians 2:3 is an example of this.

Second Thessalonians 2:3 is an end-time apostasy that occurs before the second coming of Christ. (Verse 1 sets the context by making specific reference to the coming of the Lord Jesus Christ.) Paul is speaking about a *distinguishable* apostasy headed by a *distinguishable* "man of lawlessness" (the Antichrist) that will take place before the *distinguishable* second coming of Christ at a *specific* point in time. The manifestation of this "man of lawlessness" in the future will be an actual historical event.

 Help your Mormon acquaintance see that the particular apostasy of 2 Thessalonians 2:3 culminates in the second coming of Christ, not in the formation of the Mormon church. Remember the importance of *context* in discussing Scripture with Mormons.

 The Bible *does not* contain promises of a restored church. A primary passage often cited by Mormons in this regard is Acts 3:20,21. While it is true that these verses make reference to Jesus remaining "in heaven until the time comes for God to restore everything, as he promised long ago through his holy prophets," this passage *is not* referring to a restoration of the church and of the true gospel through Joseph Smith following a total apostasy.[7]

There are several generally accepted interpretations for Acts 3:20,21. Many evangelical Christians believe the reference deals with a restoration of Israel. After all, Peter *is* speaking specifically to the "men of Israel" (see Acts 3:12) about the fulfillment of all the prophets had foretold (verse 18). The Jews had long expected Israel's restoration, and this was a central theme of the Old Testament prophets (see Isaiah 40:9-11; Jeremiah 32:42-44; Ezekiel 37:21-28; Hosea 11:9-11; 14:4-7; Amos 9:11-15). Peter may well have this Jewish restoration in view here.[8]

Other evangelical Christians take the reference to "restoration" or "restitution" more generally. These individuals believe "the restitution" follows the second coming of the Lord and deals with the consummation of the age when the Lord makes all things new (see 2 Peter 3:13).[9]

Regardless of which interpretation is correct, Acts 3:20,21 and the surrounding context *does not* even hint that there would be a *total* apostasy of the church. This is confirmed by Jesus Himself when He said to Peter: "You are Peter, and on this rock I will build my church, and *the gates of Hades will not overcome it*" (Matthew 16:18, emphasis added). To say the entire church went into complete apostasy after the death of the last apostle directly conflicts with this verse.

Scripture Interprets Scripture

A good interpretive principle is that "Scripture interprets Scripture." By consulting other Scriptures in the Bible and comparing them with one another, it becomes clear that there will never be a total apostasy of the entire church.

Jesus promised His followers, "Surely I am with you always, to the very end of the age" (Matthew 28:20). Help your Mormon friend see that Jesus could not possibly be with His followers "to the end of the age" if the entire church went into complete apostasy after the death of the last apostle. In Jesus' words we find not even a hint that the entire church would fall away from Him. His words indicate that *His sustaining power would be with His followers* to the very end!

The apostle Paul also indicates there would not be a total apostasy in the early church. In Ephesians 3:21 Paul said, "To him [God] be glory in the church and in Christ Jesus *throughout all generations*, for ever and ever" (emphasis added). How could God be glorified in the church "throughout all generations" if the entire church fell into total apostasy after the death of the last apostle? Nothing would be more unglorifying to God than a totally apostate church. Further, Ephesians, especially verses 11-16, speaks of the Christian church growing to spiritual *maturity*, not spiritual degeneracy.

The Mormon claim of restoring the Melchizedek priesthood cannot be true because this priesthood belongs only to Christ. In Psalm 110:4 we read, "The LORD has sworn and will not change his mind: 'You are a priest forever, in the order of Melchizedek.'" This is repeated in Hebrews 5:6. Mormons believe these verses prove the Melchizedek priesthood is an *eternal* priesthood, and that, today, this priesthood exists only in the Mormon church.[10]

In response, Psalm 110 is clearly a *messianic* psalm prophetically pointing to the person and work of Jesus Christ: as *king* (verses 1-3), as *priest* (verse 4), and as *a victorious warrior* (verses 5-7). Hebrews 5–8 and other New Testament passages apply Psalm 110 *to Christ alone*, not to human pretenders to the divine priesthood. Jesus quoted Psalm 110 in demonstrating that He—as the divine Messiah—was David's Lord (Mark 12:36).

When the text says that Christ is a "priest forever, in the order of Melchizedek," it is indicating that Christ's priesthood is *permanent*. As an irrevocable priest, Jesus *once for all* sacrificed Himself by His death on the cross (Hebrews 7:27,28; 10:10).

Mormons often cite Psalm 110:4 in arguing that the Melchizedek priesthood is for today because it is said to be an "eternal" priesthood. Point out that there is not a single example anywhere in the New Testament of a believer *ever* being ordained to the Melchizedek priesthood—other than the exception of the God-man, Jesus Christ. None of the disciples or apostles were *ever* ordained to this priesthood. Nor is there a single command or injunction anywhere in the New Testament instructing believers to seek ordination into this priesthood.

An important passage to share with your Mormon acquaintance is Hebrews 7:23,24, which speaks of human priests prevented from continuing in office because of death, but "because Jesus lives forever, he has a permanent priesthood." Christ's priesthood is eternal because He is *an eternal being*. His priesthood by its very nature is different than anything humans could offer. Jesus is our high priest who lives forever.

Consider the word "permanent" in Hebrews 7:24: "Because Jesus lives forever, he has a *permanent* priesthood" (emphasis added). In the Greek, this word communicates the idea of untransferable. It indicates that the priesthood is *unchangeable* and, therefore, does not pass to a successor. Do not allow the Mormon to sidestep the teaching of this verse. Christ's priesthood is "unchangeable" in the sense that it is *without successors, intransmissible,* and *untransferable.*

Christ's Priesthood Relationship

You might also want to quote Hebrews 7:11,12 to the Mormon in arguing for the passing away of the Aaronic priesthood: "If perfection could have been attained through the Levitical priesthood (for on the basis of it the law was given to the people), why was there still need for another priest to come—one in the order of Melchizedek, not in the order of Aaron? For when there is a change of the priesthood, there must also be a change of the law." Here is a clear statement from Scripture that there was a change in the priesthood. The Aaronic priesthood was done away with and replaced with something *better*—the priesthood of Jesus Christ, our *eternal* priest. This passing away of the Aaronic or Levitical priesthood was symbolized by the tearing of the veil leading to the Holy of Holies in the temple at the crucifixion (see Matthew 27:51).

Be sure to point out that Mormons are *not* descendants of Aaron (a key requirement for the Aaronic priesthood—see Numbers 3:6-12). Moreover, the duties Mormons engage in as related to their version of the Aaronic priesthood bear no resemblance to the duties of the priesthood, including offering sacrifices, as outlined in Exodus, Leviticus, Numbers, and Deuteronomy.

History disproves the claim that the Mormon church is the restored church. By tracing the history of the Christian church, it becomes clear that the Mormon claim of a "restoration" is pure fiction. Because church history is well preserved, we have an accurate picture not only regarding the teachings of the early church, but also of the deviations from orthodoxy that took place—including Gnosticism, Arianism, and Sabellianism. If it were true that Mormonism is the "restored" church, we would certainly expect to find evidence in the first century for such unique doctrines as the plurality of gods, men becoming gods, and God the Father having once been a man. But we do not find even a hint of any of these in ancient church history.

 The Mormon church has in recent years sought to downplay its exclusivism as the "restored" church. Indeed, the Mormon church has increasingly become involved with the Interfaith movement, joining with various Christian denominations in various charities. Of course, Mormons recognize that it would be very difficult for them to continue to pursue working relationships with Protestants, Catholics, and others with their historical claim that theirs is the *only* true church and all others are *apostate*. Hence, in recent years the Mormon church has softened its stance on this claim. Some Mormon leaders are now denying that Mormonism has the harsh view of orthodox Christianity for which it is known.[11]

In order to make this denial plausible, however, Mormon scholars have had to adopt strained interpretations of founder Joseph Smith's "only true church" statements.[12] For example, according to the canonized version of Joseph Smith's account of his First Vision (in which he allegedly beheld God the Father and Jesus Christ), Smith reports what he was told in response to his inquiry regarding which church he should join: "I was answered that I must join none of them, for they were all wrong; and the Personage who addressed me said that all their creeds were an abomination in his sight, that those professors were all corrupt."[13]

One conciliatory Mormon leader offered the following explanation of Joseph Smith's words: "By reading the passage carefully, we find that the Lord Jesus Christ was referring only to that particular group of ministers in the Prophet Joseph Smith's community who were quarreling about which church was true."[14]

Mormon revisionist argumentation fails. If the previous explanation were correct, all Joseph Smith had to do was move to a neighboring community and seek out a minister who was not corrupt. It would not have been necessary to completely "restore" the church of Jesus Christ on earth by founding the Mormon church. This is an important point to emphasize to your Mormon acquaintance.

The Mormon church is not the restored church.

✓ There was no total apostasy following the death of the last apostle.

✓ Since there was no total apostasy, there is no need for a "restored" church.

✓ The Aaronic priesthood passed away with the coming of Christ and is never to be restored.

✓ The Melchizedek priesthood belongs *only* to Jesus Christ.

✓ History disproves the claim that the Mormon church is the restored church.

For further information on refuting the claim that the Mormon church is the "restored" church, consult *Reasoning from the Scriptures with the Mormons,* pp. 41-61.

The Book of Mormon

Is Man-Made

Joseph Smith once said the Book of Mormon is "the most correct of any book on earth, and the keystone of our religion, and a man would get nearer to God by abiding by its precepts, than by any other book."[1] The Book of Mormon is allegedly an abridged account of God's dealings with the original inhabitants of the American continent from about 2247 B.C. to A.D. 421. Mormons claim it was originally engraved on gold plates by ancient prophets in the language of "Reformed Egyptian," deposited in a stone box, and buried in the Hill Cumorah in New York. It is said to be God's uncorrupted revelation to humankind, the "fullness of the everlasting gospel," and "another Testament of Jesus Christ." Smith is said to have "translated" the Book of Mormon from the gold plates using a "seer stone." David Whitmer, one of Smith's associates, describes the translation process:

> Joseph Smith would put the seer stone into a hat, and put his face in the hat, drawing it closely around his face to exclude the light; and in the darkness the spiritual light would shine. A piece of something resembling

parchment would appear, and on that appeared the writing. One character at a time would appear, and under it was the interpretation in English. Brother Joseph would read off the English to Oliver Cowdery, who was his principal scribe, and when it was written down and repeated to Brother Joseph to see if it was correct, then it would disappear, and another character with the interpretation would appear. Thus the Book of Mormon was translated by the gift and power of God, and not by any power of man.[2]

Following the translation of the Book of Mormon, Smith said he heard a voice from out of a bright light above him that said, "These plates have been *revealed by the power of God*, and they *have been translated by the power of God. The translation of them which you have seen is correct,* and I command you to bear record of what you now see and hear"[3] (emphasis added). In view of this precise and exact process, a process that involved *individual characters, specific words*, and alleged *direct confirmation from God,* it would seem there is room for no human error in the Book of Mormon.

Mormons believe the Bible prophesies about the Book of Mormon. Indeed, they believe the two sticks mentioned in Ezekiel 37:16,17 refer to the Bible and the Book of Mormon: "Son of man, take a stick of wood and write on it, 'Belonging to Judah and the Israelites associated with him.' Then take another stick of wood, and write on it, 'Ephraim's stick, belonging to Joseph and all the house of Israel associated with him.' Join them together into one stick so that they will become one in your hand. When your countrymen ask you, 'Won't you tell us what you mean by this?' say to them, 'This is what the Sovereign LORD says: I am going to take the stick of Joseph—which is in Ephraim's hand—and of the Israelite tribes associated with him, and join it to Judah's stick, making them a single stick of wood, and they will become one in my hand'" (Ezekiel 37:16-19). This serves to add authority to the Book of Mormon.

Be aware that Mormons often cite James 1:5 to encourage people on the doorstep to pray about the Book of Mormon and ask God if it is true: "If any of you lacks wisdom, he should ask God, who gives generously to all without finding fault, and it will be given to him." Potential converts are assured that God will show them the book is true. (More on this verse later.)

Book of Mormon

- Mormons believe the Book of Mormon is the most correct of any book on earth.

- This book is supposedly an account of God's dealings with the original inhabitants of the American continent from about 2247 B.C. to A.D. 421.

- Joseph Smith translated the Book of Mormon from golden plates by means of a "seer stone."

- Mormons believe the Bible prophesies about the Book of Mormon.

Mormons must be shown that the Book of Mormon is man-made and should not be trusted. The evidence shows that 1) there have been thousands of changes introduced into the Book of Mormon since the time of its original publication; 2) there are numerous plagiarisms in the Book of Mormon; 3) there is no archeological support for the Book of Mormon; 4) the Bible does not prophesy about the Book of Mormon; 5) the Book of Mormon contradicts current Mormon doctrine; and 6) people should *not* pray about whether the Book of Mormon is true.

There have been thousands of changes introduced into the Book of Mormon. History proves there have been more than 3,913 changes between the original edition of the Book of Mormon published in 1830

and the ones printed and issued through the mid-1970s. The 1981 edition introduced between one and two hundred additional word changes.[4] Though many of the changes relate to spelling and grammar, some are quite substantial. For example, in 1 Nephi 11:21 the phrase "Behold the Lamb of God, yea, even the eternal Father" is changed to "Behold the Lamb of God, yea even *the son of* the *eternal Father*" (emphasis added).

Constant Changes

Steve Benson, the grandson of the late Mormon leader Ezra Taft Benson, wrote the following in a newspaper article: "Troubling to us was the pathological unwillingness of the Mormon Church to deal forthrightly with its doctrine and history. Our personal study revealed that church canon, history, and scripture had been surreptitiously altered, skewed, rewritten, contradicted, and deleted."[5]

The Mormon account of how Smith went about translating the Book of Mormon disallows *any* possibility of errors—even relating to misspellings and grammar. The translation process involved Smith using a "seer stone" through which he would see *one character at a time* and read it aloud to Oliver Cowdery, after which Cowdery would repeat the character to ensure accuracy, and then that character would disappear and another would appear in its place. *Every letter and word was allegedly given by the power of God.*[6]

 Ask your Mormon acquaintance if he or she really wants to base his or her salvation on a book that has had over 4,000 changes introduced into it since its initial publication.

 Mormons may respond that there are scribal errors, typographical errors, and contradictions in the Bible, too. If they argue in this way, make the following points.

1). Citing errors in manuscript copies of the Bible should not be a smokescreen to divert attention away from the fact that the method used for translating the Book of Mormon (using seer stones, translating one character at a time) does not allow for any errors whatsoever. Insist on having an explanation for the 4,000 changes in the Book of Mormon.

2) As pointed out in chapter 3, there are only 40 or so significant variants in the manuscript copies of the Bible, and *none* of these affects any doctrine or moral commandment of Christianity. Further, unlike the situation with the Book of Mormon, there are virtually thousands of biblical manuscripts that can be objectively studied and compared by linguistic scholars to ensure accuracy. The Book of Mormon does not have that support.

3) Many thousands of archeological discoveries by both Christian and non-Christian archeologists prove the accuracy of the Bible. No such discoveries support the Book of Mormon. (See chapter 3.)

4) As scholars probe into alleged contradictions in the Bible, they consistently see that they are all explainable in a reasonable way. For example, did Judas die by hanging himself or by having his intestines burst open (see Matthew 27:5 and Acts 1:18)? This looks like a contradiction. In reality, these verses are *partial* accounts, neither one giving us the *full* picture. Taken together, we can easily reconstruct how Judas died. He hanged himself, and sometime later the rope loosened and he fell to the rocks below, causing his intestines to gush out. (See my book *The Complete Book of Bible Answers* for explanations for many "alleged" contradictions.)

There are numerous plagiarisms in the Book of Mormon. The Book of Mormon is also undermined by the many plagiarisms it contains from the King James Version of the Bible. In fact, the Book of Mormon has some 27,000 words directly from the King James

Version (KJV). For example, there are whole chapters that have been lifted from the book of Isaiah.

Even the italicized words from the KJV were included in the Book of Mormon. This is relevant because, as noted in the preface of the KJV, these words were not in the original languages but were added by the KJV translators to provide clarity. How could the Book of Mormon be written long before the KJV but contain the King James' translators' "inserted clarifying words"?

 If the Book of Mormon was first penned between 600 B.C. and A.D. 421, as claimed, how could it contain such extensive quotations from the A.D. 1611 KJV (using archaic King James English), which was not written until more than 1,000 years later?[7]

There have also been charges through the years that Smith may have borrowed from other extant sources of his day. Some believe he plagiarized from Solomon Spaulding, a retired minister who wrote two fictional narratives about the early inhabitants of America. This can't be proved or disproved because the particular book from which the Book of Mormon was allegedly plagiarized is missing. As Ruth Tucker in her book *Another Gospel* explains, "This missing volume, known as *Manuscript Found*, was, as the theory goes, left in a print shop where it was stolen by Sidney Rigdon, a close associate of Smith in the early days of Mormonism. Spaulding died in 1816, fourteen years before the Book of Mormon was published, but his stories had not been forgotten."[8] He had apparently told stories of Nephi and Lehi to customers in his tavern, and this material allegedly later found its way into the Book of Mormon. Mormons have made great efforts to discredit this. Without more evidence, the issue is still open to debate.

Others have suggested Smith may have borrowed from a book by Ethan Smith entitled *View of the Hebrews*, which held that the American Indians had Hebraic origins. Critic Fawn Brodie notes that "it may never be proved that Joseph [Smith] saw *View of the Hebrews* before writing the *Book of Mormon,* but the striking parallelisms between the books hardly leave a case for mere coincidence."[9]

Taken together, the evidence indicates that Joseph Smith drew heavily from various sources for his book. For this reason, the book cannot be trusted as revelation from God.

 There is no archeological support for the Book of Mormon. According to Mormon scriptures, the Nephite and Lamanite nations had huge populations that lived in large, fortified cities. They waged large-scale wars with each other for hundreds of years, culminating in a conflict in which hundreds of thousands of people were killed in A.D. 385, near Hill Cumorah in present-day New York State (see Mormon 6:9-15, Book of Mormon). One would think that if this really happened there would be archeological evidence to support it. But there is no evidence that it occurred. While there is massive archeological evidence to support the people and places mentioned in the Bible, such evidence is completely missing in regard to the Book of Mormon and other Mormon scriptures.

America has been studied so thoroughly by non-Mormon archeologists that one of them certainly would have come forward by now with evidence in support of the Book of Mormon if what is in the Book of Mormon is really true. But that has not happened. Archeological institutions have certainly found no support for Mormon claims. The National Museum of Natural History, Smithsonian Institution, in Washington, D.C., affirmed, "Smithsonian archeologists see no direct connection between the archeology of the New World and the subject matter of the book [of Mormon]."[10]

Similarly, the Bureau of American Ethnology asserted, "There is no evidence whatever of any migration from Israel to America, and likewise no evidence that pre-Colombian Indians had any knowledge of Christianity or the Bible."[11] In a February 4, 1982, letter, the National Geographic Society stated:

"Although many Mormon sources claim that the Book of Mormon has been substantiated by archeological findings, this claim has not been verified scientifically."[12]

In an article published in *Dialogue: A Journal of Mormon Thought*, Dee Green, assistant professor of Anthropology at Weber State College, said: "The first myth we need to eliminate is that Book of Mormon archeology exists....If one is to study Book of Mormon archeology, then one must have a corpus of data with which to deal. We do not....No Book of Mormon location is known with reference to modern topography. Biblical archeology can be studied because we do know where Jerusalem and Jericho were and are, but we do not know where Zarahemla and Bountiful (nor any other location for that matter) were or are."[13]

Many Mormon scholars try hard to find Book of Mormon lands somewhere in Central America. These scholars, however, disagree among themselves about where in Central America the Book of Mormon lands may be (some say the Costa Rica area, others say the Yucatan Peninsula, and still others say the Tehuantepec area). The fact remains there is virtually no solid archeological support for the Book of Mormon's history.

If there were large-scale wars culminating in a conflict in which hundreds of thousands of people were killed in A.D. 385 near Hill Cumorah in New York, why hasn't any archeological evidence—from non-Mormon archeologists—been revealed that such a conflict occurred?

The Bible does not prophesy about the Book of Mormon. Mormons are practicing fanciful *eisogesis* (reading a meaning into the text of Scripture) instead of *exegesis* (drawing the meaning from the text of Scripture) in claiming that the Bible prophesies the Book of Mormon. Let us consider one of their primary proof texts, Ezekiel 37:16,17:

> Son of man, take a stick of wood and write on it, "Belonging to Judah and the Israelites associated with him." Then take another stick of wood, and write on it, "Ephraim's stick, belonging to Joseph and all the house of Israel associated with him." Join them together into one stick so that they will become one in your hand.

Mormons think this passage points to the Bible and the Book of Mormon. They believe the sticks mentioned in this passage are pieces of wood around which a papyrus scroll was wrapped. "In ancient times it was the custom to write on parchment and roll it on a stick. Therefore, when this command was given, it was the equivalent of directing that two books or records should be kept."[14] One of the sticks (Judah) is allegedly referring to the Bible; the other (Joseph) is allegedly referring to the Book of Mormon.

Contrary to such a claim, the context clearly defines what the two "sticks" are. Ezekiel 37:22 says, "I will make them *one nation* in the land, on the mountains of Israel. There will be *one king* over all of them and they will *never again be two nations* or be *divided into two kingdoms*" (emphasis added). The sticks are not two books but are *two* kingdoms.

 Following Solomon's death, Israel split into two smaller kingdoms (931 B.C.). The southern kingdom was called Judah; the northern kingdom was called Israel (or sometimes Ephraim). Israel was taken into captivity by Assyria (722 B.C.); Judah was taken into exile by Babylon (605, 597, and 586 B.C.). The division between the kingdoms, however, was not to last forever. The uniting of the "sticks" pictures God's restoring His people, the children of Israel, into a single nation again (Ezekiel 37:18-28). In view of this, it is clear that the Bible *does not* prophesy about the Book of Mormon. Go over this carefully with your Mormon acquaintance.

The Book of Mormon contradicts current Mormon doctrine. The Book of Mormon, the "keystone" of the Mormon religion, contains very little in terms of "Mormonism" as taught by the Mormon church today. Among other things, the Book of Mormon says nothing about—

1. Mormon church organization
2. the Aaronic priesthood
3. the Melchizedek priesthood
4. the "plurality of gods" doctrine
5. the "God is an exalted man" doctrine
6. the doctrine that men may become gods
7. the doctrine of three degrees of glory or three kingdoms
8. the "plurality of wives" doctrine
9. the "Celestial Marriage" doctrine with all the elaborate temple ceremonies and oaths
10. baptism for the dead
11. the "word of wisdom" doctrine
12. the doctrine of preexistence
13. the doctrine of eternal progression

(*Many of these doctrines will be discussed later in this book.*)

In view of the fact that many of Mormonism's key doctrines are nowhere to be found within the pages of the Book of Mormon, how can it be claimed that the Book of Mormon is the "fullness of the everlasting gospel"?

The Book of Mormon also contains teachings that present-day Mormonism does not hold to. For example:

- Instead of teaching that there are many gods, the Book of Mormon teaches that there is only one God (Mosiah 15:1-5; Alma 11:28,29; 2 Nephi 31:21).

- Instead of teaching that people evolve to godhood, the Book of Mormon teaches that God is unchanging (Mormon 9:9,19; Moroni 8:18; Alma 41:8; 3 Nephi 24:6).

- Instead of teaching that God is a physical, exalted man, the Book of Mormon teaches that God is a spirit (Alma 18:24-28; 22:9-11).

- Though current Mormon leaders do not teach polygamy, both Joseph Smith and Brigham Young (the two greatest leaders in Mormon history) taught polygamy, even though the Book of Mormon condemned the practice (Jacob 1:15; 2:23,24,27,31; 3:5; Mosiah 11:2,4; Ether 10:5,7).

 The Book of Mormon has *many* ideas that directly contradict present-day Mormon beliefs. Is the Book of Mormon wrong or the present-day Mormon leadership?

 People should not pray about whether the Book of Mormon is true. In James 1:5 we read, "If any of you lacks wisdom, he should ask God, who gives generously to all without finding fault, and it will be given to him." Earlier I warned that Mormons often appeal to this verse in asking people to pray about the Book of Mormon to see if it is true (Moroni 10:4,5).

However, the Mormon interpretation jerks this verse out of its context. The meaning of James 1:5 is connected to the preceding verses which speak about the purpose of trials (verses 2-4). James anticipates that some of his readers will say they cannot discover any divine purpose in their trials. In that case, they are to ask God for wisdom.

Test for Truth

Prayer is not a test for religious truth. We are instructed by the apostle Paul in 1 Thessalonians 5:21 to objectively "test everything," not pray to receive a subjective feeling that something is true. Though the Bereans believed in prayer, their barometer for truth was Scripture (Acts 17:10-12). We should follow their example.

Further, even if James is not referring to gaining wisdom about the purpose of trials but is rather talking about wisdom in general, God's "wisdom" on a matter never contradicts what He has recorded in Scripture. For this reason, one need not pray about matters that God has already given us His verdict on. One does not need to pray about whether to commit murder, commit adultery, commit incest, terrorize a playground, and the like, for God's mind on such issues is clear from Scripture. One does not need to pray about whether to worship another god because the true God has already said it is wrong (Exodus 20:3). One does not need to pray about whether to participate in spiritism because God has already said it is wrong (Deuteronomy 18:9ff.). Likewise, we need not pray about the Book of Mormon because God has already condemned all gospels that contradict the Bible (Galatians 1:6-8).

 When asked to pray about the Book of Mormon, ask: Which Book of Mormon do you want me to pray about? The 1830 edition? The 1921 edition? Or today's edition, which has over 4,000 changes from the original 1830 edition? Then use this as a "launch pad" to point out the folly of trusting one's eternal salvation to a book with so many changes.

You can also point out that we need not pray about what God has already condemned.

The Book of Mormon Is Man-Made

✓ Unlike the Bible, thousands of changes have been made in the Book of Mormon since the time of its original publication.

✓ The Book of Mormon contains plagiarism.

✓ There is no objective archeological support for the Book of Mormon.

✓ The Bible does not prophesy about the Book of Mormon.

✓ The Book of Mormon contradicts current Mormon doctrine.

For further information on refuting the legitimacy of the Book of Mormon, consult *Reasoning from the Scriptures with the Mormons*, pp. 87-133.

The Bible

Is God's Word and Is Trustworthy

The Mormons' eighth "Article of Faith" affirms: "We believe the Bible to be the Word of God, as far as it is translated correctly."[1] Mormons believe that because of poor transmission, large portions of the Bible have been lost through the centuries. They also believe the portions of the Bible that have survived have become corrupted because of faulty handling.

While Mormons acknowledge that the original manuscripts penned by biblical authors were the Word of God, they aver that what passes as "the Bible" today is corrupt. It can only be trusted insofar as "it is translated correctly." Mormon apostle Orson Pratt once went so far as to ask, "Who, in his right mind, could, for one moment, suppose the Bible in its present form to be a perfect guide? Who knows that even one verse of the Bible has escaped pollution?"[2]

Joseph Smith is credited with the "translation" of the "Inspired Version of the Bible." Actually, Smith did not come up with a new translation but rather took the King James Version (KJV) and added to and subtracted from it—not by examining Bible manuscripts, but allegedly by "divine inspiration." Smith "corrected, revised, altered, added to, and deleted from" the KJV.[3]

Virtually thousands of changes were introduced. While it took a large group of the world's greatest Bible scholars (who knew Hebrew and Greek) years to finish their work on the KJV, it took Smith a mere three years to complete his work—despite the fact that he had virtually no knowledge of the biblical languages. Smith even added a passage in Genesis 50 that predicted his own coming: "That seer will I bless...and his name shall be called Joseph...."[4]

 Some Mormons, in arguing against the exclusivity of the Bible, make much of the fact that the Bible mentions specific books that are not contained in the Bible as Scripture. Luke 1:1(KJV), for example, says that "many have taken in hand to set forth in order a declaration of those things which are most surely believed among us." There is also a reference to the Book of Jashar (Joshua 10:13; 2 Samuel 1:18) and the Book of the Wars of the LORD (Numbers 21:14). Mormons conclude that these are lost books of the Bible. Of course, one implication of this is that not *all* of God's Word is in the Bible. This opens the door for Mormons to argue that other books, such as the Book of Mormon, are Scripture, too.

 ### Mormon View of the Bible

- Mormons believe the Bible is the Word of God, but only insofar as it is translated correctly.

- Due to poor transmission, large portions of the Bible have been lost. Today's Bible has many corruptions.

- Joseph Smith "corrected, revised, altered, added to, and deleted from" the KJV and called it the "Inspired Version."

- Mormons often argue that there are lost books of the Bible, which opens the door for acceptance of the Book of Mormon (and other Mormon books).

Mormons must be shown that the Bible is trustworthy.
The evidence indicates that 1) the Bible is inspired and inerrant; 2) the Bible enjoys strong manuscript support, making Mormon claims of poor transmission through the centuries false; 3) the Bible has strong archeological support; 4) the Mormon claim that there are "lost books of the Bible" is incorrect; 5) Joseph Smith's "Inspired Version" is unreliable; and 6) Joseph Smith took authority over the Bible that not even Jesus Christ claimed.

 The Bible is inspired and inerrant. Inspiration does not mean the biblical writer just felt enthusiastic, like the composer of "The Star-Spangled Banner." Nor does it mean the writings are necessarily inspiring to read, like an uplifting poem. The biblical Greek word for inspiration literally means "God-breathed." Because Scripture is breathed out by God, *because it originates from Him*, it is true and inerrant.

Biblical inspiration may be defined as God's superintending of the human authors so that, using their own individual personalities, they composed and recorded without error His revelation to humankind in the words of the original autographs. In other words, the original documents of the Bible were written by men, who, though permitted to exercise their own personalities and literary talents, wrote under the control and guidance of the Holy Spirit, the result being a perfect and errorless recording of the exact message God desired to give to mankind.

The writers of Scripture were not mere writing machines. God did not use them like keys on a typewriter to mechanically reproduce His message. Nor did He dictate the words letter by letter, page by page. The biblical evidence makes it clear that each writer had a style of his own. (Isaiah had a powerful literary style; Jeremiah had a mournful tone; Luke's style had medical overtones; and John was very simple in his approach.) The Holy

Spirit infallibly worked through each of these writers to inerrantly communicate His message to humankind.

The Bible Is Inerrant

Major Premise: God is true (Romans 3:4).

Minor Premise: God breathed out the Scriptures (2 Timothy 3:16).

Conclusion: The Scriptures are true (John 17:17).

Second Peter 1:21 provides a key insight regarding the human-divine interchange in the process of inspiration. This verse informs us that "prophecy [or Scripture] never had its origin in the will of man, but men spoke from God as they were carried along by the Holy Spirit." The phrase "carried along" in this verse literally means "forcefully borne along."

The human wills of the authors were not the originators of God's message. God did not permit the will of sinful human beings to misdirect or erroneously record His message. Rather, "God moved and the prophet mouthed these truths; God revealed and man recorded His word."[5]

Interestingly, the Greek word for "carried along" in 2 Peter 1:21 is the same as that found in Acts 27:15-17. In this passage the experienced sailors could not navigate the ship because the wind was so strong. The ship was being *driven*, *directed*, and *carried along* by the wind. This is similar to the Spirit's *driving*, *directing*, and *carrying* the human authors of the Bible as He wished. The word is a strong one, indicating the Spirit's complete superintendence of the human authors. Yet, just as the sailors were active on the ship (though the wind, not the sailors, ultimately controlled the ship's movement), so the human authors were active in writing as the Spirit directed. This is in keeping with the fact that many Old Testament passages quoted in the New Testament are said to have the Holy Spirit as their author, even though a human prophet actually spoke the words (see Mark 12:36; Acts 1:16; 28:25; Hebrews 3:7; 10:15,16).

Inerrancy Means...

The Scriptures (the Bible) possess the quality of freedom from error. They are exempt from liability of mistakes and incapable of error. In all their teachings they are in perfect accord with the truth.

Orson Pratt's comment that it is doubtful whether a single verse from the Bible can be trusted contains a fatal flaw. Indeed, even as he disparages the Bible he is casting aspersions on the Book of Mormon since it contains massive plagiarism from the Bible. And, in almost every case, the quotations contain the exact same meaning as that found in the Bible. The Bible cannot be discredited, like Pratt did, without casting doubt on the Book of Mormon.

If a Mormon to whom you are speaking says that certain parts of the Bible are unreliable, here is what I suggest: Ask him to specifically point out *all* the verses in the Bible that contain mistakes, and tell him you will avoid those verses in the discussion that will follow. Almost without exception, the Mormon will not be able to point to a specific verse. But if they do cite a verse or two, stay away from those verses and base your ensuing discussion on other verses. Let the Mormon know that since they mentioned *only* these verses (or no verses at all), the rest of the Bible is fair game for discussion.

The Bible enjoys strong manuscript support, making Mormon claims of poor transmission through the centuries false. The Book of Mormon history lacks any manuscript evidence whatsoever, whereas the Bible is supported by virtually thousands upon thousands of reliable manuscripts. There are more than 24,000 partial and complete manuscript copies of the New Testament. These manuscript copies are very ancient and available for inspection *now*.

In the many thousands of manuscript copies we possess of the New Testament, scholars have discovered that there are some 200,000 "variants." This may seem like a staggering figure to the uninformed mind. But to those who study the issue, the numbers are not as harsh as it may initially appear. For one thing, if 100 fourth-century scribes copied a third-century manuscript that contained a single variant, that would be counted as 101 variants. Every time a variant is duplicated, it counts as *another* one. So, the "200,000" number can be be misleading, since there are so many duplicates in this figure.

Further, out of these variants, 99 percent hold virtually no significance whatsoever. Many of these simply involve a missing letter in a word; some involve reversing the order of two words (such as "Christ Jesus" instead of "Jesus Christ"); some may involve the absence of one or more insignificant words. When all the facts are put on the table, only around 40 of the variants have any real significance—and even then no doctrine of the Christian faith or any moral commandment is affected by them.

By practicing the science of textual criticism—comparing all the available manuscripts with each other—we can know with a high degree of accuracy what the original document likely said.

 Use an illustration. Let us suppose we have five manuscript copies of an original document that no longer exists. Each of the manuscript copies are different. Our goal is to compare the manuscript copies and ascertain what the original said. Here are the five copies:

Manuscript 1: Jesus Christ is the Savior of the whole world.

Manuscript 2: Christ Jesus is the Savior of the whole world.

Manuscript 3: Jesus Christ s the Savior of the whole worl.

Manuscript 4: Jesus Christ is th Savior of the whle world.

Manuscript 5: Jesus Christ is the Savor of the whole wrld.

Could you, by comparing the manuscript copies, ascertain what the original document said? This illustration is simplistic, but a majority of the variants are solved by this methodology. By comparing the various manuscripts, all of which contain minor differences, it becomes fairly clear what the original must have said.

Quotes from Church Fathers

There are some 86,000 quotations of the New Testament in the writings of the early church fathers. In fact, there are enough quotations from the early church fathers that even if we did not have a single Bible manuscript, scholars could still reconstruct all but 11 verses of the New Testament.

The Dead Sea Scrolls *prove* the accuracy of the transmission of the Old Testament books of the Bible. In these scrolls, discovered at Qumran in 1947, we have Old Testament manuscripts that date about 1,000 years earlier than the other Old Testament manuscripts previously in our possession (which date to A.D.

980). The significant thing is that when one compares the two sets of manuscripts, it is clear there are very few changes. The fact that manuscripts separated by 1,000 years are essentially the same indicates the incredible accuracy of manuscript transmission.

The copy of the book of Isaiah discovered at Qumran illustrates this accuracy. Dr. Gleason Archer, who personally examined both the A.D. 980 and 150 B.C. copies of Isaiah, comments: "Even though the two copies of Isaiah discovered in Qumran Cave 1 near the Dead Sea in 1947 were a thousand years earlier than the oldest dated manuscript previously known (A.D. 980), they proved to be word for word identical with our standard Hebrew Bible in more than 95 percent of the text. The 5 percent of variation consisted chiefly of obvious slips of the pen and variations in spelling."[6]

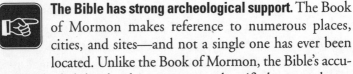 **The Bible has strong archeological support.** The Book of Mormon makes reference to numerous places, cities, and sites—and not a single one has ever been located. Unlike the Book of Mormon, the Bible's accuracy and reliability has been proven and verified over and over again by archeological finds by both believing *and* nonbelieving scholars and scientists. This includes verification for numerous customs, places, names, and events mentioned in the Bible.

Bible scholar Donald J. Wiseman notes, "The geography of Bible lands and visible remains of antiquity were gradually recorded until today more than 25,000 sites within this region and dating to Old Testament times, in their broadest sense, have been located."[7] Nelson Glueck, a specialist in ancient literature, did an exhaustive study and concluded: "It can be stated categorically that no archaeological discovery has ever controverted a biblical reference."[8] Well-known scholar William F. Albright, following a comprehensive study, wrote: "Discovery after discovery has established the accuracy of innumerable details, and has brought increased recognition of the value of the Bible as a source of history."[9]

 The Mormon claim that there are "lost books of the Bible" is false. Simply because a book is cited in the Bible does not mean that book *belongs in* the Bible as Scripture. The Bible even quotes from pagan poets and philosophers, but that does not mean these writings are inspired or belong in the Bible as Scripture (see Acts 17:28; Titus 1:12). The same is true in regard to quoting nonbiblical books.

The mere drawing of a particular fact from a book simply means that the nonbiblical book included a true fact that warranted inclusion in a biblical book. The Holy Spirit so superintended the biblical writer that he was led to select a particular true fact from a *noninspired, nonbiblical* book and include it in the *inspired* writing of a biblical book.

 If the Mormon brings up this argument while speaking to you, point out that if these books belonged in the Bible, as they claim, then God could have restored them to the Bible when Joseph Smith— under "divine inspiration"—corrected the King James Version of the Bible. But Smith *did not* "restore" them.

 Joseph Smith's "Inspired Version" is unreliable. There are numerous ways to show the unreliability of Joseph Smith's "Inspired Version" of the Bible. To begin with, it is a real stretch to argue that while it took a large group of the world's greatest Bible scholars years to finish their work on the King James Version, it took Joseph Smith a mere three years to complete his work, despite the fact he had virtually no knowledge of biblical languages. Further, the fact that Smith added a passage in Genesis 50 that predicted his own coming is preposterous.

Perhaps most problematic for Mormons is the fact that Smith's revisions to the King James text *fail to agree* with the same passages quoted in the Book of Mormon. Other portions of the Inspired Version contradict current Mormon doctrine. Hence, as apologists David A. Reed and John R. Farkas point out, a full endorsement of the Inspired Version by the Mormon Church "could prove embarrassing, but flatly rejecting it as erroneous would discredit Smith as a prophet. Instead, LDS leaders have sidestepped the issue by alleging that the work Smith began in 1831 was left unfinished at his untimely death in 1844; numerous errors remain in the uncorrected portions of the King James text, and therefore publication would be inappropriate."[10] However, Smith wrote a letter dated July 2, 1833, in which he flatly stated that he "this day finished the translating of the Scriptures."[11]

 Joseph Smith claimed authority over Scripture that not even Jesus Christ claimed. Jesus, in Matthew 5:18, said, "I tell you the truth, until heaven and earth disappear, not the smallest letter, not the least stroke of a pen, will by any means disappear from the Law until everything is accomplished." Jesus considered the Word of God as absolutely authoritative. He dared not change it. Yet Joseph Smith claimed that authority.

When Jesus was being tempted by the devil for 40 days, the devil misquoted Scripture in an attempt to thwart Christ. Christ responded by consistently pointing to the absolute authority of Scripture by saying, "It is written..." (Matthew 4:4,7,10). Jesus said, "Scripture cannot be broken" (John 10:35). Jesus used Scripture as the final court of appeal in every matter under dispute—not just with the devil, but with the Pharisees, the scribes, the Sadducees, and others.

 Some of the changes Joseph Smith made to the Bible are found in the book of Revelation. For example,

Revelation 19:15 in the King James Version says, "And out of his mouth goeth a sharp sword, that with it he should smite the nations: and he shall rule them with a rod of iron..." Joseph Smith changed this to say, "And out of his mouth proceedeth the word of God, and with it he will smite the nations; and he will rule them with the word of his mouth..." Changing the Word of God is dangerous. After all, in Revelation 22:18,19 we read: "I warn everyone who hears the words of the prophecy of this book: If anyone adds anything to them, God will add to him the plagues described in this book. And if anyone takes words away from this book of prophecy, God will take away from him his share in the tree of life and in the holy city, which are described in this book." Ask your Mormon friend about this passage.

The Bible Is God's Word and Is trustworthy

✓ The Bible is inspired by God and is, therefore, inerrant.

✓ The Bible has strong manuscript support with highly accurate transmission.

✓ The Bible has strong archeological support.

✓ The claim that there are "lost books of the Bible" is false.

✓ Joseph Smith's "Inspired Version" is untrustworthy.

For further information on refuting the Mormon view of the Bible, consult *Reasoning from the Scriptures with the Mormons*, pp. 135-86.

4

The One True God

Is an Eternal
Spirit Being

Mormon prophets and apostles teach that God the Father was once a mortal man who continually progressed to become a god (an exalted man). Mormon general authority Milton R. Hunter said that "God the Eternal Father was once a mortal man who passed through a school of earth life similar to that through which we are now passing. He became God—an exalted being—through obedience to the same eternal Gospel truths that we are given opportunity today to obey."[1] Today, then, "God the Eternal Father, our Father in Heaven, is an exalted, perfected, and glorified Personage having a tangible body of flesh and bones."[2]

Mormons often cite verses from the Bible to prove God is a physical being. For instance, it is suggested that since Adam was a physical being and was created in the "image of God" (Genesis 1:26,27), God too must have a physical body. This physicality is also "evident" in the fact that Moses spoke to God "face to face" (Exodus 33:11). Further, since Jesus (a physical being) said, "Anyone who has seen me has seen the Father" (John 14:9), the Father must have a physical body.

Joseph Smith on God

Joseph Smith said that if you were to see the Father today, "you would see him like a man in form....He was once a man like us; yea...God himself, the Father of us all, dwelt on an earth, the same as Jesus Christ himself did" (Joseph Smith, *History of the Church*, 6:305).

Mormon View of God

- God the Father was once a mortal man who continually progressed to become a god (an exalted man).
- The Father has a tangible body of flesh and bones.

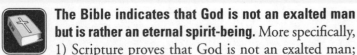

The Bible indicates that God is not an exalted man but is rather an eternal spirit-being. More specifically, 1) Scripture proves that God is not an exalted man; 2) Scripture proves that God is an eternal being; and 3) Scripture verses Mormons cite to prove God is a physical being are misinterpreted.

Scripture proves God is not an exalted man. There are many passages in Scripture which assert that God is not a man—*or* an exalted man. In Hosea 11:9 we find God affirming, "For I am God, and not man." Numbers 23:19 tells us that "God is not a man...." Romans 1:22,23 KJV says of idolaters, "Professing themselves to be wise, they became fools, and changed the glory of the incorruptible God into an image made like to corruptible man." Isaiah 45:12 quotes God as saying, "I have made the earth, and created man upon it." (Note the distinction between the *Creator* and the *creature*.) These and other verses prove beyond any doubt that God is not now nor ever has been a man.

Scripture also indicates that God, unlike man, is *invisible*. He cannot be seen. First Timothy 1:17 refers to God as "the

King eternal, immortal, invisible, the only God." Colossians 1:15 speaks of "the invisible God." John 1:18 tells us, "No one has ever seen God [the Father], but God the One and Only [Jesus Christ], who is at the Father's side, has made him known." God's invisibility is in keeping with the fact that He does not have a physical body.

If your Mormon friend has a Book of Mormon on hand, sit down and look up the following verses that indicate God is not a glorified man but rather a spiritual being:

• *Alma 22:10:* "And Aaron said unto him: Yea, he is that Great Spirit, and he created all things both in heaven and in earth. Believest thou this?"

• *Alma 31:15:* "Holy, holy God; we believe that thou art God, and we believe that thou art holy, and that thou wast a spirit, and that thou art a spirit, and that thou wilt be a spirit forever."

Be careful. You do not want to imply to the Mormon that you give credence to the Book of Mormon. Your only point is that current Mormon doctrine is not consistent with the Book of Mormon.

Scripture proves that God is an eternal being. God didn't come into being at a specific point in time, as Mormons teach. God is *beyond time* altogether. He is "the eternal King" (Jeremiah 10:10) and the "King eternal, immortal" (1 Timothy 1:17). He is "from all eternity" (Psalm 93:2). He is the one "who lives forever" (Isaiah 57:15) and is "from everlasting" (Habakkuk 1:12).

The God of the Bible is "the Eternal God" (Genesis 21:33; Deuteronomy 33:27; Romans 16:26). He is "the everlasting God" (Isaiah 40:28) and "the Rock eternal" (Isaiah 26:4). He is "from everlasting to everlasting" (1 Chronicles 16:36; Nehemiah

9:5). He perpetually remains "the same" and His years "will never end" (Psalm 102:25-27). He is the first and the last (Isaiah 44:6).

The psalmist affirmed to God, "Before the mountains were born or you brought forth the earth and the world, from everlasting to everlasting you are God" (Psalm 90:2). "The LORD is enthroned as King forever" (Psalm 29:10). God's throne "will last for ever and ever" (Psalm 45:6), and endures "from generation to generation" (Lamentations 5:19). We are assured that "God is our God for ever and ever" (Psalm 48:14). "His ways are eternal" (Habakkuk 3:6).

As an eternal being, God is not subject to change in His being, nature, and attributes. Theologians call this God's "immutability." God Himself affirmed, "I the LORD do not change" (Malachi 3:6; see also James 1:17). The psalmist declared, "You [God] remain the same, and your years will never end" (Psalm 102:27).

Even the Book of Mormon says God does not change: "For I know that God is...neither a changeable being; but he is unchangeable from all eternity to all eternity" (Moroni 8:18). Ask your Mormon friend how this verse reconciles with the current Mormon view that God was once a man and evolved to godhood.

Be careful. Again, you do not want to imply that you give credence to the Book of Mormon. Your only point is that Mormon doctrine is not consistent with the Book of Mormon.

The Scripture verses Mormons cite to prove God is a physical being are misinterpreted. Let us consider the three primary passages they cite in this regard—Genesis 1:26,27; Exodus 33:11; and John 14:9.

Genesis 1:26,27

> Then God said, "Let us make man in our image, in
> our likeness, and let them rule over the fish of the sea and
> the birds of the air, over the livestock, over all the earth,
> and over all the creatures that move along the ground." So
> God created man in his own image, in the image of God
> he created him; male and female he created them.

Mormons argue that because man was created with a flesh
and bone body, God the Father must have a physical body, too,
since man was created in God's image.[3]

A fundamental interpretive principle is that *Scripture inter-prets Scripture*. When other Scriptures about God's nature are
consulted, the Mormon understanding of Genesis 1:26,27
becomes impossible. John 4:24, for example, indicates that God
is spirit. Luke 24:39 tells us that a spirit does not have flesh and
bones. Our conclusion must be that since God is spirit, He does
not have flesh and bones. Moreover, as pointed out above, God
is not—and never has been—a man (see Hosea 11:9; Numbers
23:19; Romans 1:22,23; Isaiah 45:12).

 Ask your friend to consider this: If God is a spirit
(John 4:24), and if a spirit does not have flesh and
bones (Luke 24:39), what can we naturally conclude
regarding whether God has a physical body?

If man was not created in God's *physical* likeness, in what
way was he made in God's image? Scripture indicates that man
was created in God's image in the sense that he is a finite
reflection of God in his rational nature (Colossians 3:10), in his
moral nature (Ephesians 4:24), and in his dominion over cre-ation (Genesis 1:27,28). In the same way that the moon reflects
the brilliant light of the sun, so finite man (as created in God's
image) is a limited reflection of God in these areas.

Exodus 33:11

> The LORD would speak to Moses face to face, as a man speaks with his friend.

Mormons believe that since Moses spoke to God "face to face," God must have a physical face and therefore a physical body.[4]

As noted previously, however, Scripture indicates that God is a spirit (see Exodus 20:4; Isaiah 31:3; John 4:24). And a spirit does not have flesh and bones (Luke 24:39). It is therefore incorrect to think of God as a physical being with a literal face.

In the Hebrew mindset, "face to face" metaphorically meant "directly" or "intimately." Moses did not see a physical body, but rather entered into God's direct presence and spoke with Him in an intimate way. Consider that even a blind person can speak "face to face" with someone else—that is, directly and personally, without ever actually seeing a face.

Vine's Expository Dictionary of Biblical Words informs us that the word "face" is used anthropomorphically of God. Anthropomorphic language metaphorically attributes human characteristics to God—face, hands, eyes, arms, and so forth. Such language is not to be taken literally. Though the Bible speaks of God *as though* He had a face, the Bible clearly teaches that God is a spiritual being and should not be depicted by any likeness whatever (Exodus 20:4).[5]

 Help your Mormon acquaintance see that there are other examples of metaphorical language used of God in the Bible. For example, Psalm 91:4 says: "He will cover you with his feathers, and under his wings you will find refuge." Are we to envision God as a giant bird with wings and feathers? Scripture often uses metaphorical language to communicate spiritual truth.

John 14:9

> Anyone who has seen me has seen the Father.

Mormons take this to mean the Father has a physical body like Jesus does.

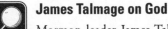

James Talmage on God

Mormon leader James Talmage said, "Even in bodily appearance the Father and the Son are alike...." Indeed, "It is clear that the Father is a personal being, possessing a definite form, with bodily parts and spiritual passions" (*A Study of the Articles of Faith,* p. 41).

Again, Scripture teaches that God is by nature spirit (John 4:24), and a spirit does not have flesh and bones (Luke 24:39). Contextually, John 14:9 simply means that Jesus is a perfect revelation of God. Earlier this same gospel said Jesus became a man specifically to reveal the Father to humankind: "No one has ever seen God, but God the One and Only [Jesus], who is at the Father's side, has made him known" (John 1:18). That is why Jesus could say, "When [a person] looks at me, he sees the one who sent me" (John 12:45). And that is why Jesus could affirm, "Whoever accepts me accepts the one who sent me" (13:20). What are some of the ways Jesus revealed the Father?

- Jesus revealed the Father's *message* to humankind: "For I did not speak of my own accord, but the Father who sent me commanded me what to say and how to say it" (John 12:49).

- Jesus' *works* served to reveal the Father: "I tell you the truth, the Son can do nothing by himself; he can do only what he sees his Father doing, because whatever the Father does the Son also does" (John 5:19).

- God's awesome *power* was revealed in Jesus (John 3:2).

- God's incredible *wisdom* was revealed in Jesus (1 Corinthians 1:24).

- God's boundless *love* was revealed and demonstrated by Jesus (1 John 3:16).

- God's unfathomable *grace* was revealed in Jesus (2 Thessalonians 1:12).

- The *glory* of God was made known by Jesus (2 Corinthians 4:6; Isaiah 40:5).

It is against this broad backdrop that Jesus said to the Jews, "Anyone who has seen me has seen the Father" (John 14:9). Jesus came as the ultimate revelation of the Father. There is nothing in this context that supports the Mormon claim that God the Father has a physical body.

God Is an Eternal Spirit

✓ God is not now or ever has been a man.

✓ God is a spirit, not a physical being.

✓ God is eternal, and He is from everlasting to everlasting.

✓ God is immutable—His nature does not change.

For further information on refuting the Mormon view of God, consult *Reasoning from the Scriptures with the Mormons,* pp. 221-41.

The Trinity

Involves
Three Persons
in One God

Mormonism teaches that the Father, Son, and Holy Spirit are not three persons *in one God,* as historic Christianity has taught, but rather that they are three separate gods. The Father, Son, and Spirit are said to be "one" only in their common purpose and in their attributes of perfection. There are many other gods as well. Spencer W. Kimball, former president of the Mormon church, made the following remarks in a priesthood meeting:

> Brethren, 225,000 of you are here tonight. I suppose 225,000 of you may become gods. There seems to be plenty of space out there in the universe. And the Lord has proved that he knows how to do it. I think he could make, or probably have us help make, worlds for all of us, for every one of us 225,000.[1]

In Mormon theology, just as Jesus has a Father, so the Father allegedly has a Father, and the Father of Jesus' Father has a Father, and so on. This endless succession of Fathers goes on and on, up the hierarchy of exalted beings in the universe. There is a Father of the Father of the Father of the Father, *ad infinitum.*

The Father Had a Father

Joseph Fielding Smith said: "If Jesus Christ was the Son of God, and John discovered that God the Father of Jesus Christ had a Father, you may suppose that he had a Father also" (*Teachings of the Prophet Joseph Smith,* p. 370).

Not only are there numerous Father-gods, there is also a heavenly wife (or wives) for each. In 1853, Mormon apostle Orson Pratt explained:

> Each God, through his wife or wives, raises up a numerous family of sons and daughters....As soon as each God has begotten many millions of male and female spirits...he, in connection with his sons, organizes a new world, after a similar order to the one which we now inhabit, where he sends both the male and female spirits to inhabit tabernacles of flesh and bones....The inhabitants of each world are required to reverence, adore, and worship their own personal father who dwells in the Heaven which they formerly inhabited.[2]

All of this is part and parcel of the polytheistic world of Mormonism. Mormons believe in numerous gods. Even though they believe the Father, Son, and Holy Spirit are the principal gods, they believe there are innumerable gods besides these. And they believe that *they, too, will one day become gods.*

Multiple Gods

Mormon apostle Orson Pratt said: "If we should take a million of worlds like this and number their particles, we should find that there are more Gods than there are particles of matter in those worlds" (*Journal of Discourses,* 2:345).

Mormon View of the Trinity

- The Trinity involves not three persons in one God but three separate gods.

- There are thousands of gods besides these three.

- Just as Jesus has a Father, so the Father has a Father, and the Father of the Father has a Father, and so on.

- Each Father-god has a heavenly wife, and together they beget many millions of male and female spirits, who can eventually become gods.

There is only one God, and He is a Trinity. More specifically, 1) the Bible refutes the polytheistic belief in many gods; 2) the Bible indicates that within the unity of the one true God are three coequal and coeternal persons—the Father, the Son, and the Holy Spirit; and 3) Mormons misinterpret certain Bible verses in support of the idea that the three persons of the Trinity are three separate gods.*

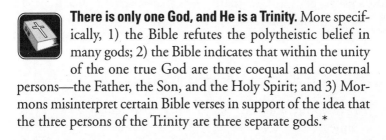

The Bible refutes the idea that there are many gods. God, through the prophet Isaiah, refuted polytheism. Because Israel was surrounded by polytheistic nations, God asked, "Is there a God beside me? yea, there is no God; I know not any" (Isaiah 44:8 KJV). If this verse is true, then God could not have had a father and a grandfather who were gods in their own rights (as Mormons teach). Otherwise, we would have to say that the God speaking in Isaiah 44:8 was either lying or forgot his own Father.

God likewise said:

- I am the first and I am the last; apart from me there is no God (Isaiah 44:6).

---

* The Bible also refutes the idea that the heavenly Father and a "heavenly mother" gave birth to spirit children, who themselves can become gods. This is discussed in chapter 6.

- I am the LORD, and there is no other; apart from me there is no God (Isaiah 45:5).

- Remember the former things, those of long ago; I am God, and there is no other; I am God, and there is none like me (Isaiah 46:9).

 Isaiah 43:10 portrays God as saying, "*Before me* there was no God formed, neither shall there be *after me*" (KJV, emphasis added). Since there were no gods *before* the God of the Bible, this means God had no Father-gods or Grandfather-gods *before* Him. Since no gods will come *after* God, this means none of His children will *become* gods. Such verses make the Mormon viewpoint impossible. Forcefully emphasize this point to your Mormon acquaintance.

Scripture uniformly teaches that *there is only one God* (see 2 Samuel 7:22; Psalm 86:10; Isaiah 44:6; James 2:19; John 5:44; 17:3; Romans 3:29,30; 16:27; Galatians 3:20; Ephesians 4:6; 1 Thessalonians 1:9; 1 Timothy 1:17; 2:5; 1 John 5:20,21; Jude 25). Deuteronomy 6:4 emphatically declares: "Hear, O Israel: The LORD our God, the LORD is one." Paul said explicitly: "We know that...there is no God but one" (1 Corinthians 8:4). In light of these verses, to agree with the Mormon viewpoint requires going against the entirety of Scripture.

 Mormons sometimes argue that they are not polytheists because polytheism is said to relate to pagan deities to whom reverence, devotion, and worship are given. Sometimes Mormons state they are not polytheists because they worship *only one* God (the Father), even though they acknowledge the existence of many gods. Do not be fooled by this semantic subterfuge. "Polytheism" comes from two Greek words—*poly* (which means "many") and *theos* (which means "God"). Polytheism means "belief in many gods."

Because Mormons believe in many gods, they are, properly speaking, *polytheists*.

 Within the unity of the one true God are three coequal and coeternal persons—the Father, the Son, and the Holy Spirit. The doctrine of the Trinity is based on three lines of evidence: 1) there is only one true God; 2) there are three persons who are God; and 3) there is three-in-oneness within the Godhead.

Evidence for One God

The fact that there is only one true God is the consistent testimony of Scripture from Genesis to Revelation. This thread of truth runs through every page of the Bible. To recap, God positively affirmed through Isaiah the prophet: "I am the first and I am the last; apart from me there is no God" (Isaiah 44:6). God said, "I am God, and there is no other; I am God, and there is none like me" (46:9). In 1 Corinthians 8:4, the apostle Paul asserted that "there is no God but one." James 2:19 affirms "there is one God." These and a multitude of other verses are clear that there is one, and *only* one, God (see, for example, John 5:44; 17:3; Romans 3:29,30; 16:27; Galatians 3:20; Ephesians 4:6; 1 Timothy 2:5).

Three Persons Who Are Called God

While Scripture is clear there is only one God, in the unfolding of God's revelation to humankind it also becomes clear that there are *three distinct persons* who are called God in Scripture.

The Father Is God

Peter refers to the saints "who have been chosen according to the foreknowledge of God the Father" (1 Peter 1:2).

Jesus Is God

When Jesus made a postresurrection appearance, doubting Thomas said, "My Lord and my God" (John 20:28). The Father said of the Son, "Your throne, O God, will last for ever and ever, and righteousness will be the scepter of your kingdom" (Hebrews 1:8).

The Holy Spirit Is God

In Acts 5:3,4, we are told that lying to the Holy Spirit is equivalent to lying to God.

Attributes of Trinity Members

Each of the three persons on different occasions are seen to possess the attributes of deity.

- All three are *omnipresent:* the Father (Matthew 19:26), the Son (Matthew 28:18), and the Holy Spirit (Psalm 139:7).

- All three are *omniscient:* the Father (Romans 11:33), the Son (Matthew 9:4), and the Holy Spirit (1 Corinthians 2:10).

- All three are *omnipotent:* the Father (1 Peter 1:5), the Son (Matthew 28:18), and the Holy Spirit (Romans 15:19).

- *Holiness* is ascribed to each person: the Father (Revelation 15:4), the Son (Acts 3:14), and the Holy Spirit (John 14:26; 16:7-14).

- *Eternity* is ascribed to each person: the Father (Psalm 90:2), the Son (Micah 5:2; John 1:2; Revelation 1:8,17), and the Holy Spirit (Hebrews 9:14).

- Each of the three is individually described as *truth:* the Father (John 7:28), the Son (John 14:6; Revelation 3:7), and the Holy Spirit (1 John 5:6).

- Each of the three is called *Lord* (Romans 10:12; Luke 2:11; 2 Corinthians 3:17), *everlasting* (Romans 16:26; Revelation 22:13; Hebrews 9:14), *almighty* (Genesis 17:1; Revelation 1:8; Romans 15:19), and *powerful* (Jeremiah 32:17; Hebrews 1:3; Luke 1:35).[3]

Works of Deity

The Father, Son, and Holy Spirit are each portrayed doing the *works* of deity. For example, all three were involved in the creation of the world: the Father (Genesis 2:7; Psalm 102:25), the Son (John 1:3; Colossians 1:16; Hebrews 1:2), and the Holy Spirit (Genesis 1:2; Job 33:4; Psalm 104:30).

Three-in-Oneness in the Godhead

Matthew 28:19 reads: "Go therefore and make disciples of all the nations, baptizing them in the name of *the* Father and *the* Son and *the* Holy Spirit" (NASB, emphasis added). It is highly revealing that the word *name* is singular in the Greek, indicating that there is one God, but three distinct persons within the Godhead—*the* Father, *the* Son, and *the* Holy Spirit.[4] Theologian Robert Reymond draws our attention to the importance of this verse for the doctrine of the Trinity:

> Jesus does not say, (1) "into the names [plural] of the Father and of the Son and of the Holy Spirit," or what is its virtual equivalent, (2) "into the name of the Father, and into the name of the Son, and into the name of the Holy Spirit," as if we had to deal with three separate Beings. Nor does He say, (3) "into the name of the Father, Son, and Holy Spirit" (omitting the three recurring articles), as if "the Father, Son, and Holy Ghost" might be taken as merely three designations of a single person. What He does say is this: (4) "into the name [singular] of *the* Father, and of *the* Son, and of *the* Holy Spirit," first asserting the unity of the three by combining them all within the bounds of the single Name, and then throwing into emphasis the distinctness of each by introducing them in turn with the repeated article.[5]

In view of the above, it is clear that the Trinity involves not three separate gods, as Mormons argue, but rather one God who is eternally manifest in three persons. We may not fully understand the Trinity, but we would have to have an infinite mind (like God) in order to fully understand God's nature. *It is not surprising that our finite minds cannot fully understand an infinite God's nature.*

 If

    1. Scripture says there is *only* one God

And

    2. Scripture calls the Father "God," calls the Son "God," and calls the Holy Spirit "God"

And

    3. Scripture in Matthew 28:19 clearly points to three-in-oneness within the Godhead

Then

    4. It is clear the Trinity involves three persons in one God, not three separate gods.

 Mormons misinterpret certain Bible verses to support the idea of three separate gods in the Trinity. Let us consider two of the passages they typically cite in this regard—Matthew 3:16,17 and Acts 7:55,56.

Matthew 3:16,17

In this passage we read:

> As soon as Jesus was baptized, he went up out of the water. At that moment heaven was opened, and he saw the Spirit of God descending like a dove and lighting on him. And a voice from heaven said, "This is my Son, whom I love; with him I am well pleased."

Mormon leader James Talmage notes that the "three personages of the Godhead were present, manifesting themselves each in a different way, and each distinct from the others."[6]

Therefore, according to Mormonism, the Father, Son, and Holy Spirit cannot be "one person," as Trinitarians believe.

 While Trinitarians believe this verse supports the doctrine of the Trinity, Mormons see three separate gods. In their attempt to disprove the evangelical viewpoint, they typically *misdefine* the Trinity as being "three in one person." Mormon missionaries often think that if they can simply show that the Father, Son, and Holy Spirit are distinct in this passage, they have proven the Trinitarian "three-in-one-person" doctrine wrong. Of course, Trinitarians do not believe the Trinity involves "three in one person." Trinitarians believe there is one God, but that within the unity of the Godhead there are three coequal and coeternal persons. (That is, there is one *what* and three *whos*.) The Trinity is not "three in one person," but "three persons in one Godhead."

It is important to understand that while Trinitarians believe Matthew 3:16,17 is *supportive* of the doctrine of the Trinity, it in itself does not *prove* the doctrine. Trinitarians base their understanding of the nature of God on the *accumulative evidence* of the whole of Scripture.

As noted earlier, some verses in the Bible clearly demonstrate the unity of God, that He is one in essence. Deuteronomy 6:4 declares: "Hear, O Israel: The LORD our God, the LORD is one." This truth of God's essential unity is repeated in the New Testament (Mark 12:29). Paul said explicitly, "We know that… there is no God but one" (1 Corinthians 8:4).

Other verses clearly show the unity *and* plurality of God. An example of this is Matthew 28:19: "Therefore go and make disciples of all nations, baptizing them in the name of the Father and of the Son and of the Holy Spirit." As noted earlier, the word *name* is singular in the Greek, indicating one God, but three distinct persons within the Godhead—*the* Father, *the* Son, and *the* Holy Spirit. Scripture taken in its *entirety* strongly points to the reality that there is one God who is eternally manifest in three persons.

Acts 7:55,56

> But Stephen, full of the Holy Spirit, looked up to heaven and saw the glory of God, and Jesus standing at the right hand of God. "Look," he said, "I see heaven open and the Son of Man standing at the right hand of God."

Mormons reason that since Stephen saw two distinct personages, with one at the "right hand" of the other, they must be distinct, separate gods.[7]

But the text does not say Stephen saw the physical, material body of God the Father. Rather, Stephen saw the "glory of God" and saw Jesus standing at the "right hand" of God.

That Stephen beheld the "glory of God" simply means that during his vision he beheld the brilliant luminosity that often accompanies divine manifestations. This is illustrated for us in the book of Isaiah. According to Isaiah 6:1-5, Isaiah beheld the incredible glory of "the LORD of hosts." The light was virtually blinding. When we get to the New Testament, in John 12:41, we are told that what Isaiah actually saw was the *glory* of Jesus Christ. The glory of God and the glory of Jesus are clearly equated here. So, when Stephen saw the "glory of God," this does not mean he saw the physical, material Father. He simply saw the brilliant luminosity that characterizes both the Father and Jesus as God.

Regarding the "right hand," this phrase does not demand that the Father has a literal body of flesh and bones. In the Jewish mind the "right hand" simply referred to the place of honor.[8] Bible expositor Ray C. Stedman notes, "The phrase *sat down at the right hand* is meant symbolically, not literally, for God has no right hand. It denotes the supreme honor accorded to the triumphant Lord, who is risen from the dead."[9] (Recall from the previous chapter that God is spirit [John 4:24], and a spirit does not have flesh and bones [Luke 24:39].)

When Stephen beheld Christ at the right hand of the Father, he witnessed Christ in His rightful place of authority, in a *position of prominence*. Any suggestion that Stephen saw two distinct, *physical* personages is unwarranted and requires reading something into the text that is not there.

Remind your Mormon acquaintance of what these verses say about the Father:

• John 1:18 says: "No one has ever seen God, but God the One and Only, who is at the Father's side, has made him known."

• 1 Timothy 1:17 tells us the Father is the "King eternal, immortal, invisible."

• Colossians 1:15 refers to the Father as "the invisible God."

Clearly, it would have been impossible for Stephen to have actually seen the Father in heaven, for God is not a physical being.

The Trinity Involves Three Persons in One God

✓ The Bible refutes polytheism.

✓ The biblical concept of the Trinity involves one God who is eternally manifest in three persons— the Father, the Son, and the Holy Spirit.

✓ Mormons misinterpret key verses to argue that the three persons of the Trinity are three separate gods.

For further information on refuting the Mormon view of the Trinity, consult *Reasoning from the Scriptures with the Mormons*, pp. 243-65.

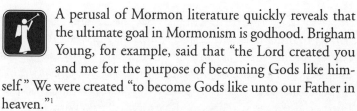

Humans

Are Creatures and Never Become Gods

A perusal of Mormon literature quickly reveals that the ultimate goal in Mormonism is godhood. Brigham Young, for example, said that "the Lord created you and me for the purpose of becoming Gods like himself." We were created "to become Gods like unto our Father in heaven."[1]

This exaltation to godhood is known as attaining "eternal life" to Mormons. The official *Gospel Principles* manual (LDS church curriculum) tells us that "exaltation is eternal life, the kind of life that God lives....We can become Gods like our heavenly Father. This is exaltation."[2] Joseph Fielding Smith said that "eternal life is the name of the kind of life possessed by the Father and the Son; it is exaltation in the eternal realm."[3]

Fundamental to understanding Mormon "exaltation" is the doctrine of *eternal progression*. The Mormon Church teaches that we do not just seek perfection in this life, it begins before birth and continues beyond the grave. Exaltation to godhood ultimately involves not just what a person does in this earthly life *(mortality)*, but what the person has already done in *premortality* ("preexistence" as a spirit child) and in *postmortality* (return to the spirit world following physical death).

A key concept related to this process relates to the word "agency," which describes each human being's right to choose between good and evil. People allegedly progress toward godhood by making "wise use" of their agency in premortality, mortality, *and* postmortality.

In premortality, spirit children (begotten by a heavenly father and heavenly mother) begin progressing toward godhood. This is a probationary period. Mormons believe the very fact that they have been born on earth is an indication that they used their agency wisely in the preexistence. It proves they did not follow Lucifer when he rebelled against God.[4] Mormons believe that such passages as Jeremiah 1:5 and John 17:5 point to the reality of human preexistence. (More on these verses later.)

Mortality, our earthly life or "Second Estate," is a *time of testing*. In order to become gods, Mormons must face (and overcome) physical temptations and trials. Obviously, as a spirit child, a person cannot be *physically* tempted because he or she has no physical body. So spirit children must take on human bodies. Further, during mortality, the Mormon is faced with an unbelievable list of requirements to progress toward godhood, including repentance, baptism, membership in the church, innumerable good works, a variety of temple rituals, and more. All of this is necessary in the Mormon system of salvation.

Regarding postmortality, Mormons say that at the moment of death a person's spirit enters the spirit world. Mormons go to a place called "paradise," where they continue in their efforts to attain godhood. Non-Mormons go to a spirit prison, where Mormon spirits evangelize them in missionary activities. If a spirit in prison accepts Mormonism, that spirit can leave the prison and enter into paradise as long as someone (a living relative) has been baptized on his or her behalf in a Mormon temple. Otherwise, the spirit is stuck in "prison" until a living relative undergoes the ritual. After entering paradise, the spirit is then free to work toward his own progression.[5]

Mormons believe the Bible supports their belief that they can become gods. Jesus, according to John 10:34, told some Jews, "You are gods." The apostle Paul in 1 Corinthians 8:5 made reference to gods in heaven and on earth. Romans 8:17 makes reference to believers as "heirs of God and co-heirs with Christ" and says believers will "share in his glory." Mormons reason that if Jesus and the chief among apostles taught the plurality of gods *and* that humans may become gods, the doctrine must certainly be true.

Mormon View of Mankind

- Human beings can be exalted to godhood.

- Attaining this lofty goal involves an extended process that spans preexistence (before being physically born on earth), mortal existence (life on earth), and post-mortal existence (afterlife).

- "Eternal progression" toward godhood hinges heavily on the right use of "agency" (choosing good over evil).

- Biblical evidence is cited that allegedly supports human deification.

The Bible is emphatic that human beings are mere creatures and never become gods.

Indeed, Scripture reveals that 1) humans are now and *forever will be* creatures in submission to the one true God; 2) Mormons misinterpret certain Bible verses as teaching human preexistence; and 3) Mormons misinterpret certain Bible verses as teaching the plurality of gods and that humans can become gods.*

---

* I will scripturally address issues related to *mortality* in chapter 8, and issues related to *postmortality* in chapter 9.

Humans are now and *forever will be* creatures in submission to the one true God. God created man out of nothing. One moment he did not exist, the next moment he did exist as a direct result of God's creative command (see Genesis 1:27; 2:7,18,20-24). Man (male and female) was created in the *image* of God (see Genesis 1:26,27), but that does not mean man *becomes* God. (Mankind simply reflects certain attributes of God in a finite way.) Scripture says that man forever remains a creature. Psalm 100:3 teaches us to "know that the LORD is God. It is he who made us, and we are his; we are his people, the sheep of his pasture." Even when man gets to heaven, he is a *redeemed* creature (see Revelation 7:9,10).

 In Acts 14, Paul demonstrated he was an uncompromising *monotheist*. After Paul healed a man in Lystra, the people started to worship him and Barnabas as gods. When Paul and Barnabas understood what was going on, "they tore their clothes and rushed out into the crowd, shouting: 'Men, why are you doing this? *We too are only men, human like you.* We are bringing you good news, telling you to turn from these worthless things to *the living God,* who made heaven and earth and sea and everything in them'" (Acts 14:14,15, emphasis added). Paul and Barnabas not only denied they were gods, they spoke of the only *true* God who created the universe. Be sure to point your Mormon acquaintance to this passage.

The attitude Paul and Barnabas displayed in Acts 14 is in obvious contrast to the folly of Herod in Acts 12:21-23. After Herod gave a public address, the people shouted, "This is the voice of a god, not of a man." Verse 23 goes on to add, "Immediately, because Herod did not give praise to God, an angel of the Lord struck him down, and he was eaten by worms and died." *God clearly does not look kindly on human pretenders to the divine throne.*

Contrary to any suggestion of humans becoming gods, the true God desires us to recognize that we are intrinsically weak, helpless, and dependent upon Him. In 2 Corinthians 3:5, the apostle Paul states, "Not that we are competent *in ourselves* to claim anything for ourselves, but our competence *comes from God*" (emphasis added). In John 15:5, Jesus affirms, "I am the vine; you are the branches. If a man remains in me and I in him, he will bear much fruit; *apart from me you can do nothing*" (emphasis added). We do not progress toward godhood; rather, as God's creatures, we are to perpetually depend upon Him.

This recognition of creaturehood should lead to humility and a worshipful attitude toward God. The psalmist tells us, "Come, let us worship and bow down, let us kneel before the LORD our Maker. For He is our God" (Psalm 95:6,7 NASB). Such humility is the mark of one who is properly related to God. Micah the prophet asks, "What does the LORD require of you but to do justice, to love kindness, and to *walk humbly* with your God?" (Micah 6:8, emphasis added). James 4:6 assures us, "God is opposed to the proud, but gives grace to the humble" (NASB).

An Unholy Desire

It is noteworthy that the perverted desire for godhood has a long history in the universe. If it is correct that Isaiah 14:12-14 and Ezekiel 28:12-19 refer to the fall of Lucifer (and there is good reason to believe this), then it seems that this was the beginning of the desire for godhood in the universe. Lucifer was originally created as the most magnificent of angels. But then an unholy desire entered his heart. Lucifer's sinful yearning is summed up in the statement, "I will make myself like the Most High" (Isaiah 14:14). Lucifer wanted to take God's place. But the only true God cast the self-inflated Lucifer from His holy presence (Isaiah 14:15).

In the Garden of Eden, Satan (Lucifer) sought to tempt Eve to eat the forbidden fruit. He enticed her by saying, "God knows that in the day you eat from it your eyes will be opened, and you will be *like* God, knowing good and evil" (Genesis 3:5, emphasis added). The fall of man was the result of this encounter. Fallen humanity—to the present day—sinfully and pridefully yearns to be "like God."

 Mormons misinterpret certain Bible verses as teaching human preexistence. Let us consider two of the primary verses Mormons cite in this regard—Jeremiah 1:5 and John 17:5.

Jeremiah 1:5

God informed Jeremiah, "Before I formed you in the womb I knew you, before you were born I set you apart; I appointed you as a prophet to the nations." Mormons believe this verse proves their doctrine of "preexistence"—the idea that human beings lived in the spirit world before being born in the flesh.[6]

Contextually, however, this verse speaks not of the soul preexisting before birth, but rather of God calling and setting apart Jeremiah for his ministry long before he was born. "I knew you" does not refer to a preexistent soul, but to the prenatal person. Jeremiah was known by God "in the womb" (see Psalm 139:13-16).

The Hebrew word for "know" *(yada)* implies a special relationship of commitment. This word is related to other words, including "sanctified" (meaning *set apart*) and "ordained," which reveal that God had a special assignment for Jeremiah even before his birth. "Know" in this context indicates God's act of making Jeremiah the special object of His sovereign choice. This verse does not imply Jeremiah's preexistence; rather, it affirms Jeremiah's *preordination* to a special ministry.

Preexistence Not Biblical

Contrary to the idea that humans preexisted as spirits, Scripture reveals that at the moment God created man, He created both his *material* aspect (body) and *immaterial* aspect (spirit). Genesis 2:7 says that "the LORD God formed the man from the dust of the ground and breathed into his nostrils the breath of life, and the man became a living being" (see also Ecclesiastes 12:7; Isaiah 42:5; and Zechariah 12:1).

John 17:5

In John 17:5 we read a portion of Jesus' "High Priestly prayer" to the Father: "And now, Father, glorify me in your presence with the glory I had with you before the world began." Mormons believe this verse supports the idea of a spirit existence prior to fleshly existence.[7]

The fundamental error in Mormon thinking is the belief that everyone—Jesus included—preexisted as literal spirit offspring of the Father, and that Jesus (the "firstborn") is our "elder brother." Scripture indicates, by contrast, that Jesus is the *only* person who preexisted. This is because He wasn't just a man; He has also existed for all eternity *as God* (John 8:58).

The Eternality of Jesus

Jesus was (is) eternal. John the Baptist said that even though Jesus in His humanity was born six months after him, as the eternal Son of God Jesus *preceded* John (John 1:30). Isaiah in his prophecy called Jesus "Everlasting Father" (Isaiah 9:6). Jesus affirmed to some Jews, "Before Abraham was born, I am" (John 8:58). Jesus thus communicated to those around Him that His human birth did not represent His actual beginnings. Indeed, He consistently startled His listeners with claims of deity and eternality.

John 3:13 tells us, "No one has ever gone into heaven except the one who came from heaven—the Son of Man." Verse 31 says, "The one who comes from above is above all; the one who is from the earth belongs to the earth, and speaks as one from the earth. The one who comes from heaven is above all." John 8:23,24 likewise says, "You are from below; I am from above. You are of this world; I am not of this world."

There is a very clear dichotomy between the *one from heaven* (Jesus) and the *ones from the earth* (humanity). If we all came from a preexistence in heaven, then these pivotal verses would have no meaning. Scripture thus negates the Mormon idea that all human beings preexisted.

 Mormons misinterpret certain Bible verses as teaching the plurality of gods *and* that humans can become gods. Let us consider three of the primary passages Mormons cite in this regard—John 10:34; 1 Corinthians 8:5; and Romans 8:16,17.

John 10:34

In this verse we find Jesus speaking to a group of Jews: "Is it not written in your Law, 'I have said you are gods'?" Mormons believe this verse proves their belief that humans can become gods.[8]

There are many reasons this text should not be used to support such a view. First, such an interpretation is contrary to the overall context. Jesus is not speaking to polytheists (who believe in many gods); rather, He is addressing strict Jewish monotheists who believe that only the Creator of the universe is God (see Genesis 1:1). Even one of the Ten Commandments points to the existence of a single God who should be worshiped (Exodus 20:4-6). So Jesus' statement should not be wrenched out of a Jewish, monotheistic context and given a polytheistic twist.

> ### Elohim
>
> Hebrew scholars tell us that the Hebrew word for "god"
> *(Elohim)* can sometimes be used of human beings. The
> judges in Psalm 82 were called "gods" *not* because they were
> actual deity but because they pronounced life and death judg-
> ments over people.

Second, Jesus' statement must be understood as part of His
overall reasoning: "If God even called human judges 'gods' (with
a small 'g'), then how much more appropriate is it that I call
Myself the Son of God, since that truly is My identity?" Christ
had just pronounced Himself one with the Father saying, "I
and the Father are one" (John 10:30). The Jews wanted to stone
Jesus because they thought He was blaspheming, making Himself out to be equal with God (verses 31-33). Jesus responded by
quoting Psalm 82:6 which says of human judges, "I have said
you are gods." Jesus thus reasoned, if human judges could be
called "gods" (in a limited sense), then why can't the Son of God
be called "God"? If these judges—by virtue of *their* work
(standing in the place of God by pronouncing life and death
decisions over people)—can be called "gods," then why can't
the Son of God, by virtue of *His* works (divine miracles), be
called "God"? It is clear from the context that these judges were
called "gods" *only* in the sense of standing in God's place,
judging over life and death matters. *They were not called "gods"
because they were divine beings.* Indeed, the text Jesus cites, Psalm
82:6, goes on to say that they were "mere men" and would in
fact "die" as men (verse 7).

Third, it is possible, as many scholars believe, that when
the psalmist Asaph said "you are gods" to the unjust judges, he
was speaking in irony. He may have been indicating to these
judges, "I have called you 'gods,' but in fact you will die like the
men you really are." If this is so, then when Jesus alluded to this
psalm in John 10, He was saying that what the Israelite judges

were called in irony and in judgment, *He is* in reality. In any event, it is clear that Jesus was giving a defense for His own deity, not for the deification of man. This verse gives no support to the Mormon view that there are many gods or that humans can become gods.

 Notice that in John 10:34 Jesus used the present tense, "you are gods." This is important because not even Mormon leaders claim they are gods at present. They believe in a *future* exaltation ("You *will be* gods"). So this verse doesn't even fit into the context of Mormon theology.

1 Corinthians 8:5

This verse makes reference to "many 'gods' and many 'lords'." Taken alone, this verse might seem to teach that there are many gods. But the context of 1 Corinthians 8 is clearly monotheistic, as the preceding verse makes clear: "We know that an idol is nothing at all in the world and that there is no God but one" (verse 4). Then, in verse 6, we read: "Yet for us *there is but one God*, the Father, from whom all things come; and for whom we live; and there is but one Lord Jesus Christ, through whom all things came, and through whom we live" (emphasis added). In verse 5, Paul is not saying there *actually are* many true "gods" and "lords"; rather, he is referring to pagan entities that some people wrongly viewed as gods and lords (such as Baal in the Old Testament).

 In the context of the city of Corinth, these "gods" were the idols of Greek and Roman mythology. Paul, in 1 Corinthians 8:5, was simply recognizing that in New Testament days many false gods were worshiped even though, in fact, such gods *did not really exist*.

Paul, as a Hebrew of Hebrews schooled in the Ten Commandments (see Exodus 20:4-6), was monotheistic to the core and believed in only one God (1 Timothy 2:5; see also Deuteronomy 6:4). Help your Mormon acquaintance understand this.

Romans 8:16,17

This passage says, "The Spirit himself testifies with our spirit that we are God's children. Now if we are children, then we are heirs—heirs of God and co-heirs with Christ, if indeed we share in his sufferings in order that we may also share in his glory." Mormons believe this passage indicates we can eventually become exalted as gods and thus have glory as gods.[9]

Contextually, this passage does not teach that humans can become exalted as gods. First of all, verse 15 indicates that believers become children of God *not by nature* but *by adoption* into God's family: "For you did not receive a spirit that makes you a slave again to fear, but you received the Spirit of sonship." Second, being a "coheir" with Christ involves not becoming exalted as a god but *inheriting* all spiritual blessings in this life (see Ephesians 1:3), and *inheriting* all the riches of God's glorious kingdom in the next life (see 1 Corinthians 3:21-23). And third, as pointed out previously, God consistently takes a strong stand against human pretenders to the divine throne (see Acts 12:22,23; see also Exodus 9:14; Acts 14:11-15).

 The only true God emphatically declared, "Before me no god was formed, nor will there be one after me" (Isaiah 43:10). This verse and others like it, such as Isaiah 44:8, completely obliterate the possibility of a human being becoming a god. Do not let your Mormon friend sidestep such verses.

Humans Are Creatures and Never Become Gods

✓ Human beings did not preexist as spirit beings.

✓ Human beings will never become gods.

✓ Human beings are finite creatures who are called to humbly submit to the infinite Creator.

For further information on refuting the Mormon view of the deification of man, consult *Reasoning from the Scriptures with the Mormons*, pp. 243-65.

Jesus

Is God—Not the Spirit-Brother of Lucifer

 According to official Mormon teaching, Jesus was begotten as the first spirit-child of the Father (Elohim) and one of his unnamed wives ("Heavenly Mother"). Jesus was allegedly the first and highest of all the spirit children. After all, He is called the "firstborn over all creation" (Colossians 1:15). Because the heavenly Father and Mother had *many* spirit children, Jesus is often referred to by Mormons as "our elder brother." (Lucifer, too, is the spirit-brother of Jesus.) Jesus progressed by obedience and devotion to the truth in the spirit world until He became God. This allegedly took eons of time. Prior to His incarnation, Jesus was the *Jehovah* of the Old Testament. (The Father, a separate God, was Elohim.)

Even though Mormons believe in innumerable gods (including Jesus), they claim they are not polytheists because they *worship* and *pray* to only one God—the Father (Elohim). They do not worship or pray to Jesus.

What this means in terms of Mormon theology is that Jesus is not really unique. The only real difference between Jesus and us is that Jesus was the *firstborn* of Elohim's children, whereas we, in our alleged preexistence, were "born" later. It appears that the important distinction between Jesus (Jehovah) and God's other premortal offspring is merely one of *degree*, not of *kind*.[1]

When it came time for his mortal birth on earth, Jesus was begotten through sexual relations between a flesh-and-bone heavenly Father and Mary. There is nothing figurative in the word "begotten." As Mormon theologian Bruce McConkie put it, "Christ was begotten by an Immortal Father in the same way that mortal men are begotten by mortal fathers."[2]

In terms of Christ's work, Mormons speak of Christ accomplishing atonement,[3] but their version of "atonement" deals only with Adam's transgression. Jesus "atoned for Adam's sin, leaving us responsible only for our own sins."[4] The Mormon's second Article of Faith affirms: "We believe that men will be punished for their own sins, and not for Adam's transgression."[5] Salvation begins with Jesus' atonement, but each person must complete the process by doing good works. The official *Gospel Principles* manual tells us that Jesus "became our savior and he did his part to help us return to our heavenly home. It is now up to each of us to do our part and to become worthy of exaltation."[6]

According to Mormon theology, the result of Jesus' atonement is that all humankind will be resurrected. Jesus was able to overcome physical death for us. He "opened the door of immortality for all to walk through. He paid the price for us to rise from the grave. Through His own willful sacrifice—the infinite and eternal atonement—we all shall live again."[7]

Mormon View of Jesus

- Jesus was "begotten" as the first spirit-child of the Father.

- Jesus was the spirit-brother of Lucifer.

- Jesus was later born on earth through physical relations between the heavenly Father and Mary.

- Jesus' atonement dealt only with Adam's transgression; we are still responsible for our own sins.
- The result of Jesus' atonement is that we will all be resurrected.

The Bible is clear that Jesus was (is) God Almighty. Indeed, Scripture proves that 1) Jesus was not procreated but is rather the *eternal* Son of God; 2) Jesus is not the spirit-brother of Lucifer; 3) Jesus is Jehovah *and* Elohim; 4) Jesus in the incarnation was not begotten by the heavenly Father and Mary, but rather the Holy Spirit overshadowed Mary; 5) Jesus as God *was* worshiped and prayed to; and 6) Jesus atoned for the sins of *all* humankind.

Jesus was not procreated but is rather the *eternal* Son of God. Ancient Semitics and Orientals used the phrase "son of…" to indicate likeness or sameness of nature and equality of being.[8] When Jesus claimed to be the Son of God, His Jewish contemporaries fully understood He was making a claim to be God in an unqualified sense (see John 5:18).[9] This is why the Jews insisted: "We have a law, and according to that law he [Christ] must die, because he claimed to be the Son of God" (John 19:7). Recognizing that Jesus was identifying Himself as God, the Jews wanted to put Him to death for blasphemy.

Evidence for Christ's eternal Sonship is found in the fact that He is represented as *already being* the Son of God before His human birth in Bethlehem (John 3:16,17). Hebrews 1:2 says God created the universe *through* His "Son"—implying that Christ was the Son of God *prior* to the Creation. Moreover, Christ *as the Son* is explicitly said to have existed "before all things" (Colossians 1:17; compare with verses 13,14). As well, Jesus, speaking as the Son of God, asserts His eternal preexistence before Abraham (John 8:58).[10]

Mormons often appeal to Psalm 2:7 in an attempt to prove Jesus was procreated by the Father.[11] However, Acts 13:33,34 makes such a view impossible, for this passage teaches that Jesus' resurrection from the dead by the Father *is a fulfillment* of the statement in Psalm 2:7: "You are my Son; today I have become your Father."[12] A basic interpretive principle is that *Scripture interprets Scripture*. The best way to find out what Psalm 2:7 means is to let Scripture *tell* us what it means. According to Acts 13:33,34 the verse deals not with the Father's alleged procreation of Jesus but rather Jesus' resurrection from the dead.

Another verse Mormons appeal to in support of the idea that Jesus was "begotten" of the Father is John 3:16, which, in the King James Version, reads: "For God so loved the world, that he gave his *only begotten Son*, that whosoever believeth in him should not perish, but have everlasting life" (emphasis added). The New International Version translates "only begotten" as "one and only," and indeed, this is what the original Greek communicates. The Greek word *monogenes* properly means "unique" or "one of a kind." It does not communicate procreation or derivation. Jesus is the *unique, one and only* "Son of God" in the sense that He has the same nature as the Father—a *divine* nature.

How are we to respond to the Mormon claim that since Jesus is called the "firstborn," He is literally Elohim's first son, "the mightiest of all the spirit children of the Father"?[13] In addition to its literal sense, Greek scholars agree that the word "firstborn" (Greek: *prototokos*) can mean "first in rank, preeminent one, heir."[14] The word carries the idea of positional preeminence and supremacy. Christ is the firstborn not in the sense that He is the first spirit-son born to Elohim, as Mormons hold, but in the sense that He is positionally preeminent over creation and is supreme over all things.[15] The backdrop is that among the ancient Hebrews, the word "firstborn" often referred to the son in the family who was in the favored position, regardless of whether or not that son was literally the first son born to the parents. This "firstborn" son would not only be the preeminent one in the family, he would also be the heir to a double portion of the family inheritance.

 This meaning of "firstborn" is illustrated in the life of King David. David was the youngest son of Jesse. Nevertheless, Psalm 89:27 says of him: "I also shall make him My first-born, the highest of the kings of the earth" (NASB). Though the *last* one born in Jesse's family, David is called the "first-born" because of the preeminent position God was placing him in.[16] Likewise, Jesus is not firstborn in the sense of "first one born," but in the sense of being preeminent over all creation (Colossians 1:15). This makes sense since Scripture says Jesus is the *Creator* of creation (Colossians 1:16).

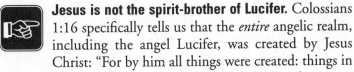 **Jesus is not the spirit-brother of Lucifer.** Colossians 1:16 specifically tells us that the *entire* angelic realm, including the angel Lucifer, was created by Jesus Christ: "For by him all things were created: things in heaven and on earth, visible and invisible, whether thrones or powers or rulers or authorities; all things were created by him and for him." The words "thrones, powers, rulers," and "authorities" were words used by rabbinical Jews in biblical times to describe different orders of angels (see Romans 8:38,39; Ephesians 1:21; 3:10; 6:12; Colossians 2:10,15).

Apparently, there was a heresy flourishing in Colossae that involved the worship of angels. In the process of worshiping angels, Christ had been degraded. To correct this grave error, Paul emphasized that Christ is the one who created all things—*including all the angels*. He is supreme and is *alone* worthy to be worshiped (see Colossians 1:16).[17]

We know from Scripture that Lucifer is a created angelic being—a "cherub" (Ezekiel 28:13-19). Since Lucifer was an angel, and since Christ created *all* the angels, it is clear that Christ is not a "spirit brother" of Lucifer. Christ is not of the created realm; rather, *He is the Creator.* Lucifer and Christ are of two entirely different classes—*creature* and *Creator*.

We see Christ's distinction from the angels (and all other creatures) stressed throughout Scripture. For example, the focus of the first three chapters of the book of Hebrews is to demonstrate the superiority of Jesus Christ—including His superiority over the *prophets* (1:1,2), over the *angels* (1:5–2:18), and over *Moses* (3:1-6).[18] How is this superiority demonstrated? Christ is shown to be God's ultimate revelation (Hebrews 3:1,2); He is the Creator and Sustainer of the universe (verses 3,4); He has the very nature of God (verse 3). None of these things could be said of mere creatures.

In Hebrews 1:6, we are specifically told that far from being in the same class as angels (such as Lucifer), Christ is worshiped *by* the angels. Angels, as *creatures*, worship Christ, the *Creator*.

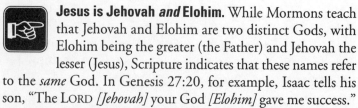

Jesus is Jehovah *and* Elohim. While Mormons teach that Jehovah and Elohim are two distinct Gods, with Elohim being the greater (the Father) and Jehovah the lesser (Jesus), Scripture indicates that these names refer to the *same* God. In Genesis 27:20, for example, Isaac tells his son, "The LORD *[Jehovah]* your God *[Elohim]* gave me success." Likewise, the Almighty Himself declares in Exodus 3:6,7:

"I am the God *[Elohim]* of your father, the God *[Elohim]* of Abraham, the God *[Elohim]* of Isaac and the God *[Elohim]* of Jacob." At this, Moses hid his face, because he was afraid to look at God *[Elohim]*. The LORD *[Jehovah]* said, "I have indeed seen the misery of my people in Egypt. I have heard them crying out because of their slave drivers, and I am concerned about their suffering."

Similarly, we read in Jeremiah 32:18: "You show love to thousands but bring the punishment for the fathers' sins into the laps of their children after them. O great and powerful God *[Elohim]*, whose name is the LORD *[Jehovah]* Almighty." We also read in Deuteronomy 6:4: "Hear, O Israel: The LORD *[Jehovah]* our God *[Elohim]*, the LORD *[Jehovah]* is one." This was a Jewish affirmation of faith in ancient days known as the *Shema*. Notice how Jehovah and Elohim are equated in this verse. Clearly there is no way to make such verses fit with the Mormon idea that Elohim is the Father and Jehovah is Jesus.

Elohim

Elohim literally means "Strong One." Elohim is portrayed in the Old Testament as the powerful and sovereign Governor of the universe, ruling over the affairs of humankind. The word "Elohim" is used to describe Him as the "God of all the earth" (Isaiah 54:5), the "God of all flesh" (Jeremiah 32:27 NASB), the "God of heaven" (Nehemiah 2:4), and the "God of gods and Lord of lords" (Deuteronomy 10:17). It is therefore highly significant that this name is used of Jesus (Isaiah 9:6; 40:3).

There are clear passages in the Bible where Jesus is individually referred to as Elohim, thereby disproving the Mormon claim that only the Father is Elohim and Jesus is Jehovah. For example, we read in Isaiah 40:3: "A voice of one calling: 'In the desert prepare the way for the LORD *[Jehovah]*; make straight in the wilderness a highway for our God *[Elohim].'*" This entire verse was written in reference to John the Baptist preparing the way for the ministry of Christ, according to John 1:22,23, and represents one of the strongest affirmations of Christ's deity in the Old Testament. Within the confines of a single verse Christ is called both Jehovah *and* Elohim.

Christ is clearly referred to as Elohim in Isaiah 9:6: "For to us a child is born, to us a son is given, and the government will be on his shoulders. And he will be called Wonderful Counselor, Mighty God *[Elohim]*, Everlasting Father, Prince of Peace." Ask your Mormon acquaintance what he or she thinks about Jesus being called Elohim in this verse.

Jesus in the Incarnation was not begotten by the heavenly Father and Mary, but rather the Holy Spirit overshadowed Mary. In Matthew 1:18-20 we read:

This is how the birth of Jesus Christ came about: His mother Mary was pledged to be married to Joseph, but before they came together, *she was found to be with child through the Holy Spirit*. Because Joseph her husband was a righteous man and did not want to expose her to public disgrace, he had in mind to divorce her quietly. But after he had considered this, an angel of the Lord appeared to him in a dream and said, "Joseph son of David, do not be afraid to take Mary home as your wife, because *what is conceived in her is from the Holy Spirit*" (emphasis added; see also Luke 1:34,35).

This passage irrefutably proves that Jesus was conceived by the Holy Spirit. Nowhere do we find any claim or evidence to the effect that the Father had physical relations with Mary—who, in Mormon theology, was the Father's "daughter."

Jesus in the Book of Mormon

Even the Book of Mormon says Jesus was conceived by the Holy Ghost. Alma 7:10 says, "And behold, he shall be born of Mary...a virgin...who shall be overshadowed and conceive by the power of the Holy Ghost, and bring forth a son, yea, even the Son of God."

Ask your friend to read aloud from Matthew 1:18-20 and, if they have a Book of Mormon on hand, Alma 7:10. Ask him or her to explain what these verses mean.

Jesus as God *was* worshiped and prayed to. Jesus was worshiped as God many times according to the Gospel accounts, and He always accepted such worship as appropriate. Jesus accepted worship from Thomas (John 20:28), the angels (Hebrews 1:6), some wise men (Matthew 2:11), a leper (Matthew 8:2), a ruler (Matthew 9:18), a blind man (John 9:38), an anonymous woman (Matthew 15:25), Mary Magdalene and "the other Mary" (Matthew 28:8,9), and the disciples (Matthew 28:16,17). All these verses contain the Greek word *proskuneo*, the same word used of worshiping the Father throughout the New Testament.

As for the Mormon claim that Jesus should not be prayed to, Mormons must be reminded of their own teaching that Jesus is the Jehovah of the Old Testament. Problematic for Mormons is the fact that numerous verses in the Old Testament command us to pray to Jehovah (Deuteronomy 4:7; 2 Chronicles 7:14; Psalm 5:2; 32:6; Jeremiah 29:7,12). If Jesus is Jehovah, and if prayers are to be offered to Jehovah, then shouldn't prayers be offered to Jesus? Furthermore, there are clear New Testament verses where prayer is made directly to Jesus (Acts 7:59; Romans 10:12).

Jesus Worshiped as God

The fact that Jesus willingly received worship says a lot about His true identity. Scripture teaches that *only God* can be worshiped. Exodus 34:14 tells us: "Do not worship any other god for the LORD, whose name is Jealous, is a jealous God." In view of this, the fact that Jesus accepted worship on numerous occasions reveals His identity as God.

Ask your friend: Did you know there are numerous verses in the Old Testament that instruct people to pray directly to Jehovah (Jesus)? (Mention Deuteronomy 4:7 and Psalm 5:2.) If prayer is not to be made to Jesus, then explain Acts 7:59 and Romans 10:12, where prayer to Jesus is clearly spoken of approvingly.

Jesus atoned for the sins of *all* humankind. Scripture portrays the death of Christ as dealing with the sins of *all* humanity, not merely the transgression of Adam.

Isaiah 53:6 says, "We all, like sheep, have gone astray, each of us has turned to his own way; and the LORD has laid on him the iniquity *of us all*" (emphasis added). In John 1:29 we read, "The next day John saw Jesus coming towards him and said, 'Look, the Lamb of God, who takes away the sin *of the world!*'" (emphasis added). First John 2:2 says, "He is the atoning sacrifice for our sins, and not only for ours but also for the sins *of the whole world*" (emphasis added).

Full Redemption in Jesus Christ

• We are *forgiven* and *redeemed* in Christ (Ephesians 1:7).
• We are *justified* in Christ (1 Corinthians 6:11).
• We are *reconciled* in Christ (Colossians 1:20).
• We are *saved* in Christ (Hebrews 7:25).

Jesus' mission was to provide a substitutionary atonement on the cross that covered the sins of *all* humanity. By so doing, He provided *total redemption* (not just resurrection from the dead) for human beings who had virtually no hope of procuring it for themselves (see Matthew 16:25,26; 26:26-28; John 12:27). It is by believing in Him alone—*with no works involved*—that a person appropriates this total redemption (John 3:16,17).

Jesus Is God, Not the Spirit-Brother of Lucifer

✓ Jesus was not procreated; He is the *eternal* Son of God.

✓ Jesus is both Jehovah *and* Elohim.

✓ The incarnation was brought about by the Holy Spirit overshadowing Mary, not by physical relations between the Father and Mary.

✓ Jesus was worshiped and prayed to as God.

✓ Jesus' full atonement for the sins of humankind provides complete redemption, not just resurrection.

For further information on refuting the Mormon view of Jesus Christ, consult *Reasoning from the Scriptures with the Mormons*, pp. 267-91.

8

Salvation

Is by Grace
Through Faith,
Not by Works

Mormons typically define "sin" as a wrong judgment, a mistake, an imperfection, or an inadequacy, thus removing the moral sting. Moreover, instead of holding to "original sin"—a doctrine that says all people are born into the world in a state of sin—Mormons say children are innocent until they reach the age of accountability, which is the age of eight. Children are said to be born innately good.[1]

With this weak view of sin, it is not surprising that Jesus' role in salvation is much reduced. In Mormonism, Jesus' atonement basically means He was able to overcome physical death for the human race. He paid the price for all people to rise from the grave. Because of what He accomplished, we will all be *resurrected*.

When Mormons talk about "salvation" (or "general salvation"), they essentially mean *resurrection*. Jesus is the "Savior" because He saved the human race from physical death. Mormons say that what Jesus did was very important because without a resurrected body one cannot become a god and give birth to spirit children.

Despite this important feat accomplished by Jesus, it did not do away with the need for good works. Indeed, Jesus did His part, and now it is up to us to do our part to prove ourselves worthy of exaltation to godhood.[2] Mormons reject the doctrine of justification by faith (which says that at the moment we believe in Jesus we are "justified" or "declared righteous" before God, without works involved).

Grace is said to be involved in Mormon salvation, but "grace" in "Mormonese" is simply God's enabling power that allows people to "lay hold on eternal life and exaltation after they have expended their own best efforts."[3] Grace aids people as they seek, by personal effort, to attain perfection (see Matthew 5:48). But God's grace *alone* does not save.[4]

The Fall a Good Thing?

Mormons believe that prior to the "fall" Adam and Eve were not yet "mortal"—meaning they did not have the capacity to bear children. After they "sinned," they attained this capacity. In a way, then, the "fall" was a good thing. Since spirit children need bodies to "progress" toward godhood, Adam's sin made it possible for them to get those needed bodies.

Biblically, God did not tell Adam and Eve they had done a good thing. Instead, He pronounced *judgment* against them and cast them out of the Garden (see Genesis 3:16-19).

Though Jesus provided "general salvation" (resurrection) for all people, to Mormons "individual salvation" refers to that which a person merits through his own acts throughout life by obedience to the laws of the gospel. Salvation in its fullest sense is synonymous with exaltation as a god and consists in gaining an inheritance in the highest of three heavens.[5] (More on these heavens in the next chapter.)

As noted earlier, exaltation to godhood in Mormon theology involves not just what is done in this earthly life *(mortality)*, but what has already been done in *premortality* ("preexistence" as a spirit child) and what is done in *postmortality* (return to the spirit world following physical death). Progression toward godhood is an extended process.

Mormon Requirements for Salvation

During mortality, there are many requirements for salvation, including:

- baptism in a Mormon church
- regular church attendance
- consistent good works
- attaining "worthiness"
- engaging in "temple work" (rituals)

During the mortal state, a person must continually work toward perfection in a physical body. In order to become a god, a Mormon must face and overcome physical temptations and trials. Obviously, as a spirit child, physical temptation is impossible because there is no physical body. Therefore, spirit children take on human bodies to progress toward godhood. Mormons cite Matthew 5:48 in support of the goal of perfection: "Be perfect, therefore, as your heavenly Father is perfect." They also cite James 2:17,26 in support of the necessity of good works in attaining salvation.

One important element in attaining salvation is baptism. Mormons often refer to Acts 2:38 in this regard: "Repent and be baptized, every one of you, in the name of Jesus Christ for the forgiveness of your sins. And you will receive the gift of the Holy Spirit."

Mormon View of Salvation

- Sin is just a wrong judgment, a mistake, an imperfection, or an inadequacy.

- There is no such thing as "original sin."

- Jesus' atonement involved overcoming physical death for the human race.

- "General salvation" refers to resurrection.

- "Individual salvation" refers to that which a person merits through his own acts throughout life by obedience to the laws of the gospel.

- Grace aids people as they seek, by personal effort, perfection.

- Baptism is necessary for salvation.

Scripture indicates that Mormons have a deficient view of sin *and* salvation. Indeed, Scripture reveals that 1) sin is an enslaving, death-producing condition involving moral rebellion; 2) sin has affected the entire human race; 3) Jesus' atonement removes the sin barrier between man and God; 4) salvation is based not upon good works but entirely upon God's grace; 5) salvation involves justification by faith; 6) perfection isn't necessary in attaining salvation; 7) good works are not required for salvation; and 8) baptism is not required for salvation.

Sin is not just a "mistake." It is an enslaving, death-producing condition involving moral rebellion against God. Though Mormons believe they have it within themselves to attain perfection and achieve exaltation as a god, Jesus' view of human sin squashes such hope. Jesus taught that man is evil (Matthew 12:34) and is capable of great wickedness (Mark 7:20-23). He said that man is lost (Luke 19:10), is a sinner (Luke 15:10), is in need of repentance before a holy God (Mark 1:15), and needs to be born again (John 3:3,5,7).

Jesus described sin as blindness (Matthew 23:16-26), sickness (Matthew 9:12), being enslaved (John 8:34), and living in darkness (John 8:12; 12:35,36). Moreover, He taught that sin is a universal condition and that *all people are guilty* (Luke 7:37-48). He also taught that both inner thoughts and external acts render a person guilty (Matthew 5:28,29). And He affirmed that God is fully aware of every person's sins; nothing escapes His notice (Matthew 22:18; Luke 6:8).

Sin has affected the *entire* human race. Contrary to Mormonism, Scripture teaches the doctrine of original sin. In Psalm 51:5 we read the words of David: "Surely I was sinful at birth, sinful from the time my mother conceived me" (compare with Psalm 53:3; Genesis 8:21). Human beings are born into the world *in a state of sin.* The sin nature is passed on from conception. This is why Ephesians 2:3 says we are "by nature objects of wrath." The apostle Paul said that "sin entered the world through one man, and death through sin, and in this way death came to all men, because all sinned" (Romans 5:12). Since Adam's time, all humans are born into the world infected by sin.

Original sin is also emphasized in Romans 5:19: "For just as through the disobedience of the one man the many were made sinners, so also through the obedience of the one man the many will be made righteous." In keeping with this, 1 Corinthians 15:21,22 tells us: "For since death came through a man, the resurrection of the dead comes also through a man. For as in Adam all die, so in Christ all will be made alive."

Jesus' atonement removes the sin barrier between man and God. The Mormon view of atonement bears little resemblance to the atonement described in the Bible. Indeed, Jesus Himself defines for us the nature of the atonement. The biblical Jesus taught that His mission was to provide a substitutionary ("die in the place of another") atonement on the cross. By so doing, He provided *total* redemption for human beings that they could not gain on their own. His atonement was not to merely provide resurrection for people, but to remove the sin barrier between man and God, thereby making it possible for people to be completely restored to God and live forever with Him in heaven.

Jesus affirmed that it was for the very purpose of dying that He came into the world (John 12:27). He also perceived His death as being a sacrificial offering for the sins of humanity and said His blood "is poured out for many for the forgiveness of sins" (Matthew 26:28). Jesus took His sacrificial mission with utmost seriousness, for He knew that without Him, humanity would perish (Matthew 16:25; John 3:16) and spend eternity apart from God in a place of great suffering (Matthew 10:28; 11:23; 23:33; 25:41; Luke 16:22-28).

Jesus described His mission this way: "The Son of Man did not come to be served, but to serve, and to give his life as a ransom for many" (Matthew 20:28). "The Son of Man came to seek and to save what was lost" (Luke 19:10). "God did not send his Son into the world to condemn the world, but to save the world through him" (John 3:17).

In John 10, Jesus compares Himself to a good shepherd who not only gives His life to save the sheep but lays His life down of His own accord (John 10:11,18). This is precisely what Jesus did at the cross (Matthew 26:53,54). He laid His life down to atone for the sins of humanity.

Certainly this is how others perceived His mission. When Jesus began His three-year ministry and was walking toward John the Baptist at the Jordan River, John said: "Look, the Lamb of God, who takes away the sin of the world!" (John 1:29). John's portrayal of Christ as the Lamb of God is a graphic affirmation that Jesus would be the sacrifice that would completely atone for the sins of humanity (see Isaiah 53:7).

Because of Jesus' atonement, restoration to God becomes a reality for all who place their faith in Christ. It is true that resurrection is a part of the overall package, but redemption is much more than that. It involves a *complete* offering whereby we are forgiven of all sins (Ephesians 1:6,7), justified or "declared righteous" (1 Corinthians 6:11), reconciled to God (Colossians 1:20), and adopted into God's forever family (Romans 8:14). Share this glorious good news with your Mormon acquaintance!

Salvation is based entirely upon God's grace. As noted earlier, in Mormon theology God's grace *alone* does not save. People must work for their ultimate exaltation. Contrary to this, the New Testament emphasizes that salvation is entirely by grace, apart from the law and good works:

- Ephesians 2:8,9: "For it is by grace you have been saved, through faith—and this not from yourselves, it is the gift of God—not by works, so that no one can boast."

- Titus 3:5: "He saved us, not because of righteous things we had done, but because of his mercy."

- Romans 3:20: "No one will be declared righteous in his sight by observing the law; rather, through the law we become conscious of sin."

- Galatians 2:16: "Know that a man is not justified by observing the law, but by faith in Jesus Christ. So we, too, have put our faith in Christ Jesus that we may be justified by faith in Christ and not by observing the law, because by observing the law no one will be justified."

Help your Mormon acquaintance see that grace (God's unmerited favor) and good works are mutually exclusive. As Romans 11:6 puts it, "If by grace, then it is no longer by works; if it were, grace would no longer be grace." It is one or the other. Salvation as defined in the New Testament is *entirely* by God's grace.

Point out that *gifts* cannot be worked for—only *wages* can be worked for. As Romans 4:4,5 tells us, "Now when a man works, his wages are not credited to him as a gift, but as an obligation. However, to the man who does not work but trusts God who justifies the wicked, his faith is credited as righteousness." Since salvation is a free gift received through faith in Christ (Ephesians 2:8,9), it cannot be earned.

Salvation involves justification by faith. Romans 3:28 tells us, "For we maintain that a man is justified by faith apart from observing the law." Romans 5:1 likewise asserts, "Therefore, since we have been justified through faith, we have peace with God through our Lord Jesus Christ." It is the *consistent* emphasis of the New Testament that salvation comes not by works but by placing personal faith in Jesus Christ. In fact, close to 200 times in the New Testament *salvation is said to be by faith alone*—with no works in sight. Here are three representative verses:

- "Everyone who believes in him may have eternal life" (John 3:15).

- "Jesus said to her, 'I am the resurrection and the life. He who believes in me will live, even though he dies'" (John 11:25).

- [Jesus says,] "I have come into the world as a light, so that no one who believes in me should stay in darkness" (John 12:46).

Help your Mormon acquaintance see that if salvation were not by faith alone, then Jesus' message in the Gospel of John would be *deceptive*, stating that there is only one condition for salvation when there are allegedly two—faith and works.

Being *justified* means we are "declared righteous" by God. Look at it this way: If we were to look through a piece of red glass, everything would appear red. If we were to look through a piece of blue glass, everything would appear blue. If we were to look through a piece of yellow glass, everything would appear yellow, and so on. Likewise, when we believe in Jesus Christ as our Savior, God looks at us *through the Lord Jesus Christ.* He sees us through the holiness of His Son.

Our sins are imputed to the account of Christ and Christ's righteousness is imputed to our account. For this reason, the Scriptures say there is now no condemnation—literally, *no punishment*—for those who are in Christ Jesus (Romans 8:1).

 Mormons misinterpret Matthew 5:48 in arguing that perfection is necessary in attaining salvation. It is true that in Matthew 5:48 Jesus said, "Be perfect, therefore, as your heavenly Father is perfect." But Jesus was not communicating that humans can attain sinless perfection in this life. Such an idea is foreign not only to the immediate context of Matthew's Gospel but to the broader context of all of Scripture.

First John 1:8 tells us: "If we claim to be without sin, we deceive ourselves and the truth is not in us." Since this epistle was written to Christians (1 John 2:12-14,19; 3:1; 5:13), it seems clear that they can never attain moral or spiritual perfection as Mormons hope.

Further, the great saints of the Bible seemed to recognize their own intrinsic sinfulness (Isaiah 6:5; Daniel 9:4-19; Ephesians 3:8). If anyone could have attained perfection, certainly

Isaiah, Daniel, and the apostle Paul would have been contenders. But none of them succeeded. Why? Because they still had the sin nature in them that continually erupted in their lives (Ephesians 2:3).

In view of humanity's dire sin problem as defined by Scripture, Matthew 5:48 cannot be interpreted to mean that humans can attain sinless perfection in this life. How, then, can we make sense of this verse? Contextually, this verse is found in a section of Scripture dealing not with the issue of sin but with the *law of love*. The Jewish leaders of Jesus' day had taught that people should love those who are near and dear to them (Leviticus 19:18), but hate those who are enemies. Jesus refuted this idea, instructing us to love even our enemies and revealing that God's love extends to *all* people (see Matthew 5:45). And since God is our righteous standard, we should seek to be as He is in this regard. We are to be "perfect" (or *complete*) in loving as He is perfect.

 Help your Mormon friend understand their present lack of perfection and the implication this has for attaining salvation. Mention that according to James 2:10, "Whoever keeps the whole law and yet stumbles at just one point is guilty of breaking all of it." With a motive of love, "drive the point home" as forcefully as you can. Help him or her see that self-effort to reach perfection is doomed to fail. Only when the Mormon realizes this will he or she recognize a need for Christ, who was perfect on our behalf and wiped away our sins by His death on the cross.

Point your Mormon acquaintance to Hebrews 10:14, which speaks of what Christ Himself has accomplished on our behalf: "By one sacrifice *he has made perfect forever* those who are being made holy" (emphasis added). Christ has done it all! Christ has "perfected forever" those who have trusted in Him. He alone takes away our imperfections (sins).

Mormons misinterpret James 2:17,26 in arguing that good works are necessary for salvation. It is true that James 2:17,26 indicates that faith without works is dead. However, as Martin Luther rightly observed, James 2 *is not* teaching that a person is saved by works. Rather a person is "justified" (declared righteous before God) by faith alone, but *not by a faith that is alone.* In other words, genuine faith will *always result* in good works in the saved person's life.

James is writing to Jewish Christians who were in danger of giving nothing but lip-service to Jesus (see James 1:1). His intent, therefore, is to distinguish true faith from false faith. He shows that true faith results in works, visible evidences of faith's invisible presence. Good works are the "vital signs" indicating that faith is alive.

Apparently some of these Jewish Christians had made a false claim of faith. "It is the spurious boast of faith that James condemned. Merely claiming to have faith is not enough. Genuine faith is evidenced by works."[6] Indeed, "workless faith is worthless faith; it is unproductive, sterile, barren, dead! Great claims may be made about a corpse that is supposed to have come to life, but if it does not move, if there are no vital signs, no heartbeat, no perceptible pulse, it is still dead. The false claims are silenced by the evidence."[7] The fact is, apart from the spirit, the body is dead; it's a lifeless corpse. Apart from the evidence of good works, faith is dead. It is lifeless and nonproductive. That is what James is teaching in this passage.

Mormons may respond by pointing to Philippians 2:12: "Continue to work out your salvation with fear and trembling." Respond by pointing out that the whole of Scripture emphasizes that works have nothing to do with salvation (see Ephesians 2:8,9; Romans 3:20,28). And, since Scripture interprets Scripture, this verse cannot be interpreted to mean we must do works in order to attain final salvation.

Many scholars believe Philippians 2:12 deals not with the assurance of final salvation for individual believers but rather with the *corporate* "salvation" of the church in Philippi. This church was suffering under intense rivalries (Philippians 2:3,4), disturbances caused by Judaizers (3:1-3), and libertinism (3:18,19). Because of these internal problems that hindered spiritual growth, the Philippian church as a whole was in need of temporal "salvation"—it needed to deal with and overcome these troubles.

 Mormons misinterpret Acts 2:38 in arguing that baptism is necessary for salvation. In this verse Peter said, "Repent and be baptized, every one of you, in the name of Jesus Christ for the forgiveness of your sins. And you will receive the gift of the Holy Spirit." Contrary to Mormon teaching, Acts 2:38 does not teach that a person must be baptized to be saved. Admittedly, this is not an easy verse to interpret, but a basic principle of Bible interpretation is that difficult passages are to be interpreted in light of the easy, clear verses.

The great majority of passages dealing with salvation in the New Testament affirm that salvation is by faith alone. A good example is John 3:16,17: "For God so loved the world that he gave his one and only Son, that whoever believes in him shall not perish but have eternal life. For God did not send his Son into the world to condemn the world, but to save the world through him." In view of such clear passages, how is Acts 2:38 to be interpreted?

A single word in the verse gives us the answer. "Repent and be baptized, every one of you, in the name of Jesus Christ *for* the forgiveness of your sins" (emphasis added). Students of the

Greek language have often pointed out that the Greek word "for" *(eis)* is a preposition that can indicate *causality* ("in order to attain") or a *result* ("because of").

An example of using "for" in a resultant sense is the sentence: "I'm taking an aspirin for my headache." Obviously this means I'm taking an aspirin as a result of my headache. I'm not taking an aspirin in order to attain a headache.

An example of using "for" in a causal sense is the sentence: "I'm going to the office for my paycheck." Obviously this means I'm going to the office in order to attain my paycheck.

Now, in Acts 2:38 the word "for" is used in a *resultant* sense. The verse might be paraphrased, "Repent, and be baptized every one of you in the name of Jesus Christ because of *(as a result of)* the remission of sins." The verse is not saying, "Repent, and be baptized every one of you in the name of Jesus Christ in order to attain the remission of sins." Hence, this verse, properly interpreted, indicates that water baptism *follows* the salvation experience.

 Mention the following words of the apostle Paul to your Mormon acquaintance: "For Christ did not send me to baptize, but to preach the gospel—not with words of human wisdom, lest the cross of Christ be emptied of its power" (1 Corinthians 1:17). Paul draws a clear distinction between baptism and the gospel. And since it is the gospel that saves (1 Corinthians 15:1,2), clearly baptism is not necessary to attain salvation.

Salvation Is by Grace Through Faith

✓ Sin involves moral rebellion against God. All of humanity is fallen in sin.

✓ Jesus, by His death, has provided a complete redemption for those who trust in Him.

✓ Works play no part in salvation.

✓ Salvation is by grace through faith.

 For further information on refuting the Mormon view of salvation, consult *Reasoning from the Scriptures with the Mormons*, pp. 311-89.

The Afterlife

Involves Heaven and Hell—Not Three Degrees of Glory

 At the end of the world, Mormons believe people will end up in one of three kingdoms of glory: the celestial kingdom, the terrestrial kingdom, or the telestial kingdom. A person's level of worthiness determines which of these three realms he or she ends up in.

The celestial kingdom is said to be the highest degree of glory, and it is inhabited by faithful Mormons—the "righteous, those who have been faithful in keeping the commandments of the Lord, and have been cleansed of all their sins."[1] Children who die before the age of eight (the age of accountability) also go there. This is the kingdom where people will live with the heavenly Father and Jesus Christ. On this level people can attain ultimate exaltation to godhood.

The second of the three degrees of glory is the terrestrial kingdom. This is reserved for non-Mormons who live moral lives as well as "less than valiant" Mormons (those who did not live up to their church's expectations or requirements).

The lowest of the three degrees of glory is the telestial kingdom, which is where the great majority of people go. It is reserved for those who have been carnal and sinful throughout life. The occupants must temporarily suffer through hell ("outer darkness") before entering. After people "suffer in full" for their sins, they are then permitted to enter into this kingdom.

Mormons believe there is support in the Bible for these three kingdoms of glory in 1 Corinthians 15:40-42 (KJV)[2]:

> There are also celestial bodies, and bodies terrestrial:
> but the glory of the celestial is one, and the glory of the
> terrestrial is another. There is one glory of the sun, and
> another glory of the moon, and another glory of the stars:
> for one star differeth from another star in glory. So also is
> the resurrection of the dead. It is sown in corruption; it is
> raised in incorruption.

Mormons also cite 2 Corinthians 12:2 in support of this doctrine: "I know a man in Christ who fourteen years ago was caught up to the third heaven. Whether it was in the body or out of the body I do not know—God knows." Mormons argue that there could not be a third heaven unless there was a first and second heaven as well.[3]

Mormon View of the Afterlife

- Mormons believe that all people end up in one of three kingdoms of glory—the celestial, the terrestrial, or the telestial.

- The celestial kingdom is the highest degree of glory and is inhabited by faithful Mormons.

- The terrestrial kingdom is reserved for non-Mormons who live moral lives as well as "less than valiant" Mormons.

- The telestial kingdom is reserved for those who have been carnal and sinful throughout life.

- Mormons appeal to 1 Corinthians 15:40-42 and 2 Corinthians 12:2 in support of these three kingdoms.

The Bible asserts that people will end up either in heaven or hell in the afterlife, depending on whether they have trusted in Christ. Indeed, Scripture rightly interpreted indicates that 1) Mormons *misinterpret* Scripture in support of the idea that there are three kingdoms in the afterlife; 2) there are only two possible destinies in the afterlife—heaven or hell; 3) *all* believers will be with Christ in heaven; and 4) *all* unbelievers will suffer for all eternity in hell.

 Mormons misinterpret Scripture in support of the idea that there are three kingdoms in the afterlife. Let us consider the two primary passages they cite in this regard— 1 Corinthians 15:40-42 and 2 Corinthians 12:12.

1 Corinthians 15:40-42

The first thing to note is that 1 Corinthians 15:40-42 does not make reference to the word "telestial." Only the words "terrestrial" and "celestial" are mentioned. This automatically disqualifies this passage as a support for the idea that there is a telestial kingdom. Mormons are reading something into the passage that simply is not there.

The context of 1 Corinthians 15:40-42 is set for us in verse 35 (KJV), where two questions are asked: "How are the dead raised up? and with what body do they come?" The rest of 1 Corinthians 15 answers these questions. Paul was talking about *resurrection bodies,* not kingdoms.

Contextually, the word "celestial" means *heavenly,* and "terrestrial" means *earthly.* Paul, in this verse, is talking about the heavenly body as opposed to the earthly body. As the passage goes on to indicate, the earthly body is fallen, temporal, imperfect, and weak (see 1 Corinthians 15:42-44). The heavenly body, by contrast, will be eternal, perfect, and powerful (see 2 Corinthians 5:1-4).

Help your Mormon acquaintance see that in 1 Corinthians 15:40-50 the apostle Paul draws a series of contrasts between the earthly body and the heavenly body: *perishable/imperishable, weak/powerful, natural/supernatural,* and *mortal/immortal.* Contextually, there is no way to read a theology of three kingdoms into a passage dealing with two kinds of bodies: the earthly body and the heavenly body. Emphasize the importance of context.

The Mormon may bring up the reference to the *sun, moon,* and *stars* in 1 Corinthians 15:41, pointing to how each of these have a different level of glory and splendor. Contextually, all Paul is saying is that the differences in splendor between *earthly* "bodies" (animals, birds, fish—see verse 39) and *heavenly* "bodies" (sun, moon, stars—verse 41) serve as an illustration of the incredible difference in splendor between an earthly *human* body and a heavenly resurrected *human* body (see Daniel 12:3; Matthew 13:43).

2 Corinthians 12:2

As noted earlier, an important interpretive principle is that Scripture interprets Scripture. By comparing various Scripture passages dealing with heaven, it quickly becomes clear what Paul is talking about in 2 Corinthians 12:2 where he refers to the "third heaven." There are, in fact, three "heavens" mentioned in the Bible—the *atmospheric* heaven (Deuteronomy 11:11), the *starry* heaven (Genesis 1:14), and the *highest* heaven—God's realm where believers go upon death (Isaiah 63:15). It is to this last heaven that Paul refers in 2 Corinthians 12:2.

By contrast, when Hebrews 4:14 speaks of Christ having "ascended higher than all the heavens," it is the atmospheric heaven and starry heaven that are referred to. Indeed, Christ dwells in the *highest* heaven (the third heaven—God's realm), and it is to that realm that the apostle Paul was caught up.

No Book of Mormon Support

The doctrine of three kingdoms of glory is not even in harmony with the Book of Mormon. According to 1 Nephi 15:35, there is only a *heaven* and a *hell.* (See also Mormon 9:23; Alma 3:26; 40:26; 41:4; Mosiah 16:11; 2 Nephi 2:28,29; 9:16; 28:21,22; 3 Nephi 27:11,17.)

There are only two possible destinies in the afterlife—heaven or hell. The Scriptures consistently categorize people into one of two classes: saved or unsaved. They portray the final destiny of every person as being one of two realities—heaven or hell. Consider these key passages:

- In Matthew 13:30, Jesus, in His parable of the wheat and tares, said, "Let both grow together until the harvest. At that time I will tell the harvesters: First collect the weeds and tie them in bundles to be burned; then gather the wheat and bring it into my barn." In this verse, believers and unbelievers are spoken of as *wheat* and *tares.* Two classes. (Note that the Bible does not speak of three categories of wheat, each going to a different barn.) All the wheat is gathered into Christ's one "barn." The "tares" are excluded and are burned.

- In Matthew 13:49,50 Jesus said, "This is how it will be at the end of the age. The angels will come and separate the wicked from the righteous and throw them into the fiery furnace." Again, two classes are mentioned—unbelievers (wicked) and believers (righteous), each with a different destiny (hell or heaven).

- In Matthew 25:32 Jesus said that following His second coming, "all the nations will be gathered before him, and he will separate the people one from another as a shepherd separates the sheep from the goats." Believers and unbelievers are differentiated by the terms "sheep" and "goats." The sheep (all of them together) will enter into God's (single) kingdom (verse 34) and inherit eternal life (see verse 46). The goats go into eternal punishment (see verse 46).

In view of such passages, it is clear there are two classes of people (the saved and the unsaved) and two possible destinies (heaven for the saved; hell for the unsaved). Each respective person ends up in one of these destinies based upon whether he or she accepted salvation through Christ during his or her time on earth (see John 3:16,17; Acts 16:31).

 ***All* believers will be in a *single* location—with Christ in heaven.** Jesus promised, "If any man serve me, let him follow me; and where I am, there shall also my servant be: if any man serve me, him will my Father honour" (John 12:26 KJV). No mention of three kingdoms here. Whoever follows Christ will be *where Christ is* (heaven). All who believe in Christ are heirs of the (singular) eternal kingdom (Galatians 3:29; 4:28-31; Titus 3:7; James 2:5). Romans 3:22 asserts that the righteousness of God that leads to life in heaven is available "unto all and upon all them that believe: for there is no difference."

 In John 10:16, Jesus affirms that all who believe in Him will be in "*one* fold" under "*one* shepherd." There will not be three separate "folds" or kingdoms. One fold, one shepherd. One kingdom, one King. Help your Mormon acquaintance grasp this important truth.

 ***All* unbelievers will suffer for eternity in hell.** The Bible reveals that those who go into eternity having rejected Jesus Christ will suffer forever in hell. There is no second chance. Contrary to the Mormon view, a person (including the *moral* person) who dies without placing saving faith in the true Jesus of the Bible will spend eternity apart from Christ in a place of great suffering.

Matthew 25:46 (KJV) tells us, "And these shall go away into everlasting punishment: but the righteous into life eternal." A critical point to make in regard to this verse is that the punishment is said to be *everlasting*. The Greek adjective *aionion* in this verse means "everlasting, without end." You might want to point out to the Mormon that this same adjective is predicated of God (the "eternal" God) in 1 Timothy 1:7; Romans 16:26; Hebrews 9:14; 13:8; and Revelation 4:9. The punishment of the wicked does not involve a temporary purging preparatory to the so-called telestial kingdom, but is rather an everlasting punishment.

The Horror of Hell

Scripture uses a variety of words to describe the horrors of hell—fire, fiery furnace, unquenchable fire, the lake of burning sulfur, the Lake of Fire, everlasting contempt, perdition, the place of weeping and gnashing of teeth, eternal punishment, darkness, the wrath to come, damnation, condemnation, retribution, woe, and the second death. Hell is a horrible destiny.

One of the more important New Testament words for hell is "gehenna" (Matthew 10:28). This word has an interesting history. For several generations in ancient Israel, atrocities were committed in the Valley of Ben Hinnom—atrocities that included human sacrifices (see 2 Chronicles 28:3; 33:6; Jeremiah 32:35). Children were sacrificed to the false Moabite god Molech. Jeremiah appropriately called this valley a "valley of slaughter" (Jeremiah 7:32). Eventually the valley came to be used as a public rubbish dump into which all the filth in Jerusalem was poured. Not only garbage but also the bodies of dead animals and the corpses of criminals were thrown onto the heap where they would be destroyed. The valley was a place where the fires never stopped burning. This place was originally called (in Hebrew) *Ge[gen]hinnom* (the valley of the sons of Hinnom). It was eventually shortened to the name *Ge-Hinnom*. The Greek translation of this Hebrew phrase is *Gehenna*. It became an appropriate and graphic metaphor for the horror of hell. Jesus used this word 11 times as a metaphorical way of describing the eternal place of suffering of unredeemed humanity.

This truth about heaven and hell has tremendous implications for our evangelism among Mormons because they worship a different God, a different Jesus, and set forth a different gospel. Unless they can be reached for Christ, they will spend eternity in this horrible place called hell. I urge you to make every effort to share the true God, the true Jesus, and the true gospel with every Mormon you come into contact with.

The Afterlife Involves Heaven and Hell Only

✓ Mormons misinterpret key New Testament passages to support their view that there are three kingdoms of glory in the afterlife.

✓ There are only two possible destinies for people in the afterlife—heaven or hell.

✓ All of God's people will be in a single location—in heaven.

For further information on refuting the Mormon view of the afterlife, consult *Reasoning from the Scriptures with the Mormons*, pp. 369-89.

Jesus
Changed
My Life
Forever

One of the ten most important things to say to a Mormon *must* include a testimony of what the Lord Jesus has done in your life. Giving your personal testimony is a very important component of any witnessing encounter, but it is especially important in the case of the Mormon. When the Mormon tries to "testify" to you that Mormonism is the truth, and that the Book of Mormon is the Word of God, you need to be ready with *your* testimony—a testimony that communicates the *real* truth sprinkled with lots of quotations from the *real* Word of God—the Bible.

In my own case, throughout my childhood and teenage years I thought I was a Christian because I regularly attended church. For years I participated in various church activities, sang in the church choir, and went through all the motions. I even went through a "confirmation" ceremony at my church—an event that was supposed to confirm that, in fact, I was a Christian. I had no idea at that time that I really was not a Christian according to the biblical definition.

Like so many others today, I was under the illusion that a Christian was a church attender or someone who basically subscribed to a Christian code of ethics. I believed that as long as I was fairly consistent in living my life in accordance with this code of ethics, I was surely a Christian. I believed that as long as my good deeds outweighed my bad deeds by the time I died, I could look forward to a destiny in heaven.

It wasn't until years later that I came to understand that the mere act of going to church did not make me a Christian. As the great evangelist Billy Sunday (1862–1935) put it, "Going to church doesn't make you a Christian any more than going to a garage makes you an automobile."[1]

Most fundamentally, a Christian is someone who has a personal, ongoing relationship with Jesus. It is a relationship that begins the moment a person places faith in Christ for salvation. Christianity is not so much a *religion* as it is a *relationship*.

It is fascinating that the word "Christian" is used only three times in the New Testament—the most important of which is Acts 11:26: "The disciples were called Christians first at Antioch" (see also Acts 26:28; 1 Peter 4:16). This would have been around A.D. 42, about a decade *after* Christ died on the cross and resurrected from the dead. Up until this time the followers of Jesus had been known among themselves by such terms as "brethren" (Acts 15:1,23), "disciples" (Acts 9:26), "believers" (Acts 5:14), and "saints" (Romans 8:27). But now, in Antioch, they are called Christians.

What does the term mean? The answer is found in the "ian" ending, for among the ancients this ending meant "belonging to the party of." "Herodians" belonged to the party of Herod. "Caesarians" belonged to the party of Caesar. "Christians" belonged to Christ. And Christians were loyal to Christ, just as the Herodians were loyal to Herod and Caesarians were loyal to Caesar (see Matthew 22:16; Mark 3:6; 12:13).

The significance of the name *Christian* was that these followers of Jesus were recognized as a distinct group. They were seen as distinct from Judaism and as distinct from all other religions of the ancient world. We might loosely translate the term Christian as "those belonging to Christ," "Christ-ones," or "Christ-people." *They are ones who follow Christ.* People who have studied the culture of Antioch have noted that the Antiochans were well known for making fun of people. It may be that the early followers of Jesus were called "Christians" by local residents as a term of derision, an appellation of ridicule. Be that as it may, history reveals that by the second century, Christians adopted the title as a badge of honor. They took pride (in a healthy way) in following Jesus. They had a genuine relationship with the living, resurrected Christ, and they were utterly faithful to Him—even in the face of death.

I bring this up because in your personal testimony to a Mormon, a pivotal part of it must be that you are *sure* of going to heaven precisely because you have a *personal relationship with Christ.* You have meaning in your present life not because you obey rules (like the massive list of rules the Mormon must heed during mortality), but because you are a Christian. Indeed, you have a *personal relationship with Christ.*

Great Christians throughout church history have long emphasized that Christianity fundamentally involves this personal relationship.

- Josiah Strong (1847–1916) said, "Christianity is neither a creed nor a ceremonial, but life vitally connected with a loving Christ."[2]

- Stephen Neill said, "Christianity is not the acceptance of certain ideas. It is a personal attitude of trust and devotion to a person."[3]

- John R.W. Stott said, "A Christian is, in essence, somebody personally related to Jesus Christ."[4] He also said, "Christianity without Christ is a chest without a treasure, a frame without a portrait, a corpse without breath."[5]

- Oswald Chambers (1874–1917) said, "Christianity is not devotion to work, or to a cause, or a doctrine, but devotion to a person, the Lord Jesus Christ."[6]

- Billy Graham said, "Christianity isn't only going to church on Sunday. It is living twenty-four hours of every day with Jesus Christ."[7]

So, again, as you give your personal testimony, a key emphasis you must continually bring up is that you are a Christian not because you do good works, not because you follow rules, not because you attend a particular church, not because you read a Bible, *but because you have a personal relationship with Jesus*, the living Lord and true God of the universe.*

Having laid this basic foundation, here are a few pointers to keep in mind regarding testimonies. These are the things I keep in mind when I tell people what the Lord has done in my own life.

 There is a strong biblical precedent for God's people telling others what God has done in their lives, and we are to follow their example. Consider:

- "Give thanks to the LORD, call on his name; make known among the nations what he has done" (1 Chronicles 16:8).

- "Tell of all his wonderful acts" (1 Chronicles 16:9).

- "Proclaim among the nations what he has done" (Psalm 9:11).

- "Let us tell in Zion what the LORD our God has done" (Jeremiah 51:10).

- "Whoever acknowledges me before men, I will also acknowledge him before my Father in heaven" (Matthew 10:32).

- "Jesus…said, 'Go home to your family and tell them how much the Lord has done for you, and how he has had mercy on you.' So the man went away and began to tell in the Decapolis how much Jesus had done for him. And all the people were amazed" (Mark 5:19,20).

- "You are witnesses of these things" (Luke 24:48).

- "Then, leaving her water jar, the woman went back to the town and said to the people, 'Come, see a man who told me everything I ever did. Could this be the Christ?' They came out of the town and made their way toward him.…

---

* Make sure the Mormon thouroughly understands Jesus' true identity as God. Otherwise, he or she may interpret "Jesus" through a Mormon grid by thinking of Jesus as an "elder brother."

Many of the Samaritans from that town believed in him because of the woman's testimony, 'He told me everything I ever did'" (John 4:28-31,39).

- "Do not be ashamed to testify about our Lord, or ashamed of me his prisoner. But join with me in suffering for the gospel, by the power of God" (2 Timothy 1:8).

- "Always be prepared to give an answer to everyone who asks you to give the reason for the hope that you have. But do this with gentleness and respect" (1 Peter 3:15).

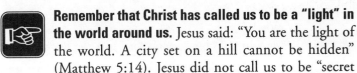 **Remember that Christ has called us to be a "light" in the world around us.** Jesus said: "You are the light of the world. A city set on a hill cannot be hidden" (Matthew 5:14). Jesus did not call us to be "secret agent" Christians. We are not to cloak our lights. Someone once said, "No one is a light unto himself, not even the sun."[8] Because the darkness of the cults is hovering over Western culture as never before, there has never been a time when the "light" of each individual Christian has been more needed. As evangelist Billy Graham put it, "The Christian should stand out like a sparkling diamond."[9]

We are called to be personal witnesses specifically of Jesus Christ. Just before ascending into heaven Jesus instructed His disciples: "You will receive power when the Holy Spirit comes upon you; and you will be my witnesses in Jerusalem, and in all Judea and Samaria, and to the ends of the earth" (Acts 1:8). A *witness* is a person who gives a testimony. Christians testify *about Jesus*—who He is, what He has done, and how people can have a personal relationship with Him.

A Christian leader once said, "Every heart *with* Christ is a missionary; every heart *without* Christ is a mission field." Christians can be witnessing missionaries wherever they are, whether it be abroad or at home. And when the opportunity arises, we must be ready to share the good news.

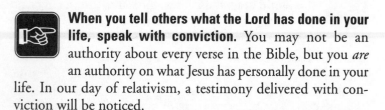

How You Live Is Important

It is not just our words that serve as a witness for Jesus. Our actions should reflect the life of Christ within us. When people around us notice this difference, it serves as a mighty witness to the joys and benefits of following Jesus. So, don't just share the *facts* of your relationship with Jesus; let your friend see the *effects* of that relationship in your life.

When you tell others what the Lord has done in your life, speak with conviction. You may not be an authority about every verse in the Bible, but you *are* an authority on what Jesus has personally done in your life. In our day of relativism, a testimony delivered with conviction will be noticed.

Be careful not to have a spiritual chip on your shoulder when you give your testimony. A spiritual chip is the communication of the feeling that you have something he or she does not have. Such an attitude will turn him or her off as fast as anything you could imagine. Christians who have thoroughly prepared themselves by learning hard-hitting scriptural answers to Mormon errors must be especially careful to come across as loving and objective. Make every effort, with God's help, to *remain humble* during your witnessing encounter. Watch out for spiritual pride—it is deadly!

When giving your testimony, be sure to share what your life was like *before* you were a Christian, *how* you became a Christian, and what your life has been like *since* becoming a Christian.

- Describe what your feelings, attitudes, actions, and relationships were like before you were a Christian. (The apostle

Paul, in his testimony, clearly spoke of what his life was like before he was a Christian in Acts 26:4-11.)

• What events led up to your decision to trust in Christ? What caused you to begin considering Christ as a solution to your needs? Be specific.

• Describe your conversion experience. Were you in a church? Were other Christians with you at the time? (The apostle Paul, in his testimony, clearly spoke of how he became a Christian in Acts 26:12-18.)

• What kind of change took place in your life following your conversion? What effect did trusting in Christ have on your feelings, attitudes, actions, and relationships? (Paul spoke of how his life changed once becoming a Christian in Acts 26:19-23.)

CAUTION

There are certain things you should avoid when sharing your personal testimony.

• *Do not be long-winded.* People have short attention spans. Unless they indicate they want every detail, cover the essential points in brief fashion.

• *Avoid overuse of "Christianese" language.* Do not use theological language your listener may be unfamiliar with, including *justification, reconciliation,* and *sanctification.* If you do use such words, be sure to clearly define what you mean by them. (Be sensitive to the fact that Mormons use many of the same biblical words we do, but they *redefine* them. This means you must clearly communicate what you mean by the words you use.)

• *Do not communicate in your testimony that true Christianity yields a bed of roses for believers.* Such a claim is simply not true. You might even share some of the struggles you have gone through since becoming a Christian. Your listener may identify with what you have experienced.

• *Do not be insensitive to the Mormon's "works" background.* The apostle Paul in 1 Corinthians 2:14 stated: "A natural man does not accept the things of the Spirit of God, for they are foolishness to him; and he cannot understand them, because they are spiritually appraised" (NASB). The gospel of God's grace may not make much sense to one who has been thoroughly schooled in a gospel that involves the necessity of works throughout life. For this reason, devote a good part of your testimony to how the gospel of God's grace has set you free—and cite lots of Scripture.

 Be sure to give the Mormon a clear picture of how to become a Christian, based on the objective Word of God. Following are important points to establish.

God Desires a Personal Relationship with Human Beings

God created human beings (Genesis 1:27). And He did not just create them to exist all alone and apart from Him. He created them with a view to being in a personal relationship with them. Just as God fellowshiped with Adam and Eve (Genesis 3:8-19), so He desires to fellowship *with us* (1 John 1:5-7). God *loves* us (John 3:16).

The problem is...

We Have a Sin Problem

When Adam and Eve chose to sin against God in the Garden of Eden, they catapulted the entire human race, to which they gave birth, into sin. Since the time of Adam and Eve, *every* human being has been born into the world with a propensity to sin. (Mormons deny the doctrine of original sin, so be ready to defend this point with plenty of Scripture.)

The apostle Paul affirmed that "sin entered the world through one man, and death through sin" (Romans 5:12). Indeed, we are told that "through the disobedience of the one man the many were made sinners" (Romans 5:19). Ultimately this means that "death came through a man...in Adam all die" (1 Corinthians 15:21,22).

Contrary to the Mormon minimalization of sin as a "mistake," Jesus often spoke of sin in metaphors that illustrate the tremendous havoc sin can wreak in one's life. He described sin as blindness (Matthew 23:16-26), sickness (Matthew 9:12), being enslaved (John 8:34), and living in darkness (John 8:12; 12:35-46). Moreover, Jesus taught that this is a universal condition and that all people are guilty before God (Luke 7:37-48).

Jesus also taught that both inner thoughts and external acts render a person guilty (Matthew 5:28). He taught that from within the human heart come "evil thoughts, sexual immorality, theft, murder, adultery, greed, malice, deceit, lewdness, envy, slander, arrogance and folly" (Mark 7:21,22). Moreover, He affirmed that God is fully aware of every person's sins, both external acts and inner thoughts. Nothing escapes His notice (Matthew 22:18; Luke 6:8; John 4:17-19).

Of course, some people are more morally upright than others. (The Mormon to whom you are speaking may well be highly moral, seeking perfection in daily life.) But even if we seek to do good works every day, we *all* fall short of God's infinite standards (Romans 3:23). In a contest to see who can throw a rock to the moon, I am sure a muscular athlete would be able to throw the rock much farther than I could. But all human beings ultimately fail in this task. Similarly, all of us fall short of measuring up to God's perfect holy standards.

The good news is that...

Jesus Made Salvation Possible!

God's absolute holiness demands that sin be punished. The good news of the gospel, however, is that Jesus has taken this punishment on Himself. God loves us so much that He sent Jesus to bear the penalty for our sins!

It is critical that you help the Mormon understand what Scripture says about this. Jesus affirmed that it was for the very purpose of dying that He came into the world (John 12:27).

Moreover, He perceived His death as being a sacrificial offering *for the sins of all humanity* (Matthew 26:26-28). (This is in contrast to the Mormon teaching that Jesus covered only Adam's transgression.) Jesus took His sacrificial mission with utmost seriousness, for He knew that without Him humanity would certainly perish (John 3:16) and spend eternity apart from God in a place of great suffering (Matthew 10:28; 11:23; 23:33; 25:41; Luke 16:22-28).

Jesus described His mission this way: "The Son of Man did not come to be served, but to serve, and to give his life as a ransom for many" (Matthew 20:28). "The Son of Man came to seek and to save what was lost" (Luke 19:10). "For God did not send his Son into the world to condemn the world, but to save the world through him" (John 3:17). And because of what Jesus accomplished on the cross for us, we have a *complete* and *wonderful redemption* (not just resurrection). (Review chapter 8 for critical information on the Mormon view of salvation.)

Emphasize to your Mormon acquaintance that the benefits of Christ's death on the cross are not automatically applied to our lives.

God requires us to...

Believe in Jesus Christ

By His sacrificial death on the cross, Jesus took the sins of the *entire world* on Himself (not just the sin of Adam) and made salvation available *for everyone* (1 John 2:2). But this salvation is not automatic. Only those who choose to believe in Christ are saved. This is the consistent testimony of the biblical Jesus. "For God so loved the world that he gave his one and only Son, that whoever *believes* in him shall not perish but have eternal life" (John 3:16, emphasis added). "I am the resurrection and the life. He who *believes* in me will live, even though he dies" (John 11:25, emphasis added).

Choosing *not* to believe in Jesus, by contrast, leads to eternal condemnation: "Whoever *believes* in him is not condemned, but whoever *does not believe* stands condemned already because he has not believed in the name of God's one and only Son" (John 3:18, emphasis added).

Free at Last: Forgiven of All Sins

When a person believes in Christ the Savior, a wonderful thing happens. God forgives him of all his sins. *All of them!* He puts them completely out of His sight. Be sure to share the following verses, which speak of the forgiveness of those who have believed in Christ:

- "In him we have redemption through his blood, the forgiveness of sins, in accordance with the riches of God's grace" (Ephesians 1:7).

- God said, "Their sins and lawless acts I will remember no more" (Hebrews 10:17).

- "Blessed is he whose transgressions are forgiven, whose sins are covered. Blessed is the man whose sin the LORD does not count against him and in whose spirit is no deceit" (Psalm 32:1,2).

- "For as high as the heavens are above the earth, so great is his love for those who fear him; as far as the east is from the west, so far has he removed our transgressions from us" (Psalm 103:11,12).

Such forgiveness is wonderful indeed. None of us can possibly work our way into salvation. Because of what Jesus has done for us, we freely receive the gift of salvation! It is provided solely through the grace of God (Ephesians 2:8,9). And it is ours by simply believing in Jesus.

Don't Put It Off

Help your Mormon acquaintance understand it is highly dangerous to put off turning to Christ for salvation, for no one knows the day of his or her death. What if it happens this evening? "Death is the destiny of every man; the living should take this to heart" (Ecclesiastes 7:2). "Seek the LORD while he may be found; call on him while he is near" (Isaiah 55:6).

A Simple Prayer of Faith

If the Mormon to whom you are speaking expresses interest in trusting in Jesus alone* for salvation, lead him or her in a simple prayer like the following. Be sure to emphasize that it is not the prayer itself that saves anyone; it is the *faith* in one's heart that brings salvation.

> *Dear Jesus,*
> *I want to have a relationship with You.*
> *I know I can't save myself because I'm a sinner.*
> *Thank You for dying on the cross on my behalf.*
> *I believe You died for me. I accept Your free gift of salvation.*
> *Thank You, Jesus!*
> *Amen.*

Welcome the Mormon into God's Forever Family

On the authority of the Word of God, you can now assure the Mormon that he or she is part of God's forever family! Encourage him or her with the prospect of spending all eternity by the side of Jesus in heaven.

 For further information on witnessing to Mormons, consult *Reasoning from the Scriptures with the Mormons*, pp. 9-21, 403-08.

Note: The Mormon you've led to Christ *still needs your help!* Help him get grounded in a good Bible-believing church. Introduce him to some of your Christian friends, and have your friends pray for him regularly. Realize that he may be carrying some psychological and spiritual "baggage" from his past association with the Mormon church. Help him work through this. See if there is a Christian support group for former Mormons in your area. Check it out and, if appropriate, refer him to it.

---

* Again, be sure the Mormon understands the true identity of Jesus—He is God, not just the spirit-brother of Lucifer.

Bibliography

Christian Critiques on Mormonism

Ankerberg, John and John Weldon. *Cult Watch: What You Need to Know About Spiritual Deception.* Eugene, OR: Harvest House Publishers, 1991.

Cares, Mark J. *Speaking the Truth in Love to Mormons.* Milwaukee, WI: Northwestern Publishing House, 1993.

Hoekema, Anthony A. *The Four Major Cults.* Grand Rapids: Eerdmans, 1978.

Martin, Walter. *The Kingdom of the Cults.* Minneapolis: Bethany House Publishers, 1985.

———. *The Maze of Mormonism.* Ventura, CA: Regal Books, 1978.

McKeever, Bill. *Answering Mormons' Questions.* Minneapolis: Bethany House Publishers, 1991.

McKeever, Bill and Eric Johnson. *Questions to Ask Your Mormon Friend.* Minneapolis: Bethany House Publishers, 1994.

Reed, David A. and John R. Farkas. *How to Rescue Your Loved One from Mormonism.* Grand Rapids, MI: Baker Book House, 1994.

———. *Mormons Answered Verse by Verse.* Grand Rapids, MI: Baker Book House, 1992.

Tanner, Jerald and Sandra. *3,913 Changes in the Book of Mormon.* Salt Lake City: Lighthouse Ministry, n.d.

———. *Archaeology and the Book of Mormon.* Salt Lake City: Modern Microfilm Company, 1969.

———. *Major Problems of Mormonism.* Salt Lake City: Lighthouse Ministry, 1989.

———. *The Changing World of Mormonism.* Chicago: Moody Press, 1981.

Tanner, Sandra. *Mormonism, Magic and Masonry.* Salt Lake City: Lighthouse Ministry, 1988.

Tucker, Ruth. *Another Gospel: Alternative Religions and the New Age Movement.* Grand Rapids, MI: Zondervan Publishing House, 1989.

Primary Mormon Publications

Benson, Ezra Taft. *The Teachings of Ezra Taft Benson.* Salt Lake City: Bookcraft, 1988.

"Bible Dictionary," in *The Holy Bible.* Salt Lake City: Church of Jesus Christ of Latter-day Saints, 1990.

Book of Mormon. Salt Lake City: The Church of Jesus Christ of Latter-day Saints, 1990.

Cannon, George Q. *Gospel Truth.* Salt Lake City: Deseret Book Company, 1987.

Doctrine and Covenants. Salt Lake City: The Church of Jesus Christ of Latter-day Saints, 1990.

Encyclopedia of Mormonism, Daniel H. Ludlow, ed. New York: Macmillan, 1992.

Gospel Principles. Salt Lake City: Church of Jesus Christ of Latter-day Saints, 1981.

Hunter, Milton R. *The Gospel Through the Ages.* Salt Lake City: Deseret Book Co., 1958.

Kimball, Edward, ed. *The Teachings of Spencer W. Kimball.* Salt Lake City: Bookcraft, 1982.

———. *The Miracle of Forgiveness.* Salt Lake City: Bookcraft, 1969.

Kimball, Spencer W. *Repentance Brings Forgiveness.* Salt Lake City: The Church of Jesus Christ of Latter-day Saints, 1984.

Matthews, Robert J. *A Sure Foundation.* Salt Lake City: Deseret, 1988.

McConkie, Bruce. *Doctrinal New Testament Commentary*, vol. 2. Salt Lake City: Bookcraft, 1976.

———. *Mormon Doctrine*, 2d ed. Salt Lake City: Bookcraft, 1977.

McKay, David O. *Gospel Ideals.* Salt Lake City: Improvement Era, 1953.

Petersen, Mark E. *As Translated Correctly.* Salt Lake City: Deseret, 1966.

Pratt, Orson. *The Seer.* Washington, D.C.: n.p., 1853-54.

Richards, LeGrand. *A Marvelous Work and a Wonder.* Salt Lake City: Deseret Book Company, 1958.

Smith, Joseph Fielding. *Doctrines of Salvation.* Salt Lake City: Bookcraft, 1975.

———. *Man: His Origin and Destiny.* Salt Lake City.

———. *The Way to Perfection.* Salt Lake City: Deseret, n.d.

Smith, Joseph. *History of the Church of Jesus Christ of Latter-day Saints.* Salt Lake City: Deseret Book Company, 1973.

Talmage, James E. *The Articles of Faith.* Salt Lake City: The Church of Jesus Christ of Latter-day Saints, 1982.

———. *The Great Apostasy.* Salt Lake City: Deseret Book Company, 1975.

Widtsoe, John A. *Evidences and Reconciliations.* Salt Lake City: Bookcraft, 1987.

———. *Joseph Smith—Seeker After Truth.* Salt Lake City: Deseret, 1951.

Young, Brigham. *Journal of Discourses.* London: Latter-day Saints' Book Depot, 1854-56.

Notes

Chapter 1

1. Joseph Smith, *History of the Church of Jesus Christ of Latter-day Saints* (Salt Lake City: Deseret Book Company, 1973), 1:17,19.
2. Joseph Fielding Smith, ed., *Teachings of the Prophet Joseph Smith* (Salt Lake City: Deseret Book Company, 1977), p. 158.
3. Bruce McConkie, *Mormon Doctrine* (Salt Lake City: Bookcraft, 1977), p. 334.
4. *New Bible Commentary*, eds. G.J. Wenham, J.A. Motyer, D.A. Carson, and R.T. France (Downers Grove, IL: InterVarsity Press, 1994), p. 1209.
5. James E. Talmage, *The Great Apostasy* (Salt Lake City: Deseret Book Company, 1975), p. 41; see also McConkie, *Mormon Doctrine*, p. 43.
6. *The Bible Knowledge Commentary*, eds. John F. Walvoord and Roy Zuck (Wheaton, IL: Victor Books, 1985), p. 718.
7. As stated in LeGrand Richards, *A Marvelous Work and a Wonder* (Salt Lake City: Deseret, 1958), p. 35.
8. Craig S. Keener, *The IVP Bible Background Commentary* (Downers Grove, IL: InterVarsity Press, 1993), p. 332.
9. Spiros Zodhiates, *The Complete Word Study Dictionary* (Chattanooga: AMG Publishers, 1992), p. 226.
10. *Doctrine and Covenants* 84:26-28.
11. Robert M. Bowman, Jr., "How Mormons Are Defending Mormon Doctrine," *Christian Research Journal*, Fall 1989, p. 26.
12. Ibid., p. 26.
13. Smith, *History of the Church*, 1:19.
14. Cited by Bowman, "How Mormons," p. 26.

Chapter 2

1. Joseph Fielding Smith, *History of the Church of Jesus Christ of Latter-day Saints* (Salt Lake City: Deseret, 1973), 4:461.
2. David Whitmer, *An Address to All Believers in Christ* (Concord, CA: Pacific, 1976), p. 12.
3. Smith, *History*, 1:54-55.
4. Scott Faulring, "Changes in New Triple: Part 1—The Book of Mormon," Seventh East Press, 21 October 1981, Provo, Utah.
5. *Arizona Republic*, 22 May 1994, p. C-1.
6. Whitmer, *Address*, pp. 12ff.
7. Jerald and Sandra Tanner, *Major Problems of Mormonism* (Salt Lake City: Utah Lighthouse Ministry, 1990), pp. 148-54.
8. Ruth Tucker, *Another Gospel* (Grand Rapids: Zondervan, 1989), p. 56.
9. Fawn Brodie, *No Man Knows My History* (New York: Knopf, 1971), pp. 46-47.
10. Cited in Tanner, *Major Problems*, p. 162.
11. Cited in John Ankerberg and John Weldon, *Cult Watch* (Eugene, OR: Harvest House, 1991), p. 38.
12. Cited in Tanner, *Major Problems*, p. 162.

13. Dee F. Green, *Dialogue: A Journal of Mormon Thought*, Summer 1969, pp. 76-78.
14. LeGrand Richards, *A Marvelous Work and a Wonder* (Salt Lake City: Deseret, 1973), p. 67.

Chapter 3

1. James E. Talmage, *A Study of the Articles of Faith* (Salt Lake City: The Church of Jesus Christ of Latter-day Saints, 1982), p. 236.
2. Orson Pratt, *Divine Authenticity of the Book of Mormon*, p. 47, cited in Bill McKeever and Eric Johnson, *Questions to Ask Your Mormon Friend* (Minneapolis: Bethany House, 1994), p. 47.
3. Bruce McConkie, *Mormon Doctrine* (Salt Lake City: Bookcraft, 1977), p. 383.
4. Joseph Smith, Genesis 40:33, Inspired Version.
5. Norman Geisler and William Nix, *A General Introduction to the Bible* (Chicago: Moody Press, 1978), p. 28.
6. Gleason Archer, *A Survey of Old Testament Introduction* (Chicago: Moody Press, 1964), p. 19.
7. Donald J. Wiseman, "Archaeological Confirmation of the Old Testament," in Norman Geisler, *Christian Apologetics* (Grand Rapids: Baker Book House, 1976), p. 322.
8. Nelson Glueck, *Rivers in the Desert* (Philadelphia: Jewish Publications Society of America, 1969), p. 31.
9. William F. Albright, cited in Josh McDowell, *Evidence That Demands a Verdict* (San Bernardino, CA: Campus Crusade for Christ, 1972), p. 68.
10. David A. Reed and John R. Farkas, *Mormons Answered Verse by Verse* (Grand Rapids: Baker Book House, 1992), p. 29.
11. Joseph Smith, *History of the Church of Jesus Christ of Latter-day Saints* (Salt Lake City: Deseret, 1973), 1:368.

Chapter 4

1. Milton R. Hunter, *The Gospel Through the Ages* (Salt Lake City: Deseret, 1958), p. 104.
2. Bruce McConkie, *Mormon Doctrine* (Salt Lake City: Bookcraft, 1977), p. 278.
3. Joseph Fielding Smith, *Doctrines of Salvation* (Salt Lake City: Bookcraft, 1975), 1:3.
4. LeGrand Richards, *A Marvelous Work and a Wonder* (Salt Lake City: Deseret, 1958), p. 16.
5. *Vine's Expository Dictionary of Biblical Words*, eds. W.E. Vine, Merrill F. Unger, and William White, eds. (Nashville: Thomas Nelson Publishers, 1985), p. 75.

Chapter 5

1. Spencer W. Kimball, *The Ensign*, Salt Lake City, Nov. 1975, p. 80. See James White, *Is the Mormon My Brother?* (Minneapolis: Bethany House Publishers, 1997), p. 105.

2. Orson Pratt, *The Seer* (Washington, D.C.: n.p., 1853-54), pp. 37-38.
3. *The New Treasury of Scripture Knowledge*, ed. Jerome Smith (Nashville: Thomas Nelson, 1995), pp. 1095-96.
4. Benjamin B. Warfield, *The Person and Work of Christ* (Philadelphia: Presbyterian and Reformed, 1950), p. 66.
5. Ibid., p. 66.
6. James Talmage, *The Articles of Faith* (Salt Lake City: Church of Jesus Christ of Latter-day Saints, 1982), pp. 39-40.
7. Ibid., p. 40.
8. Charles C. Ryrie, *The Ryrie Study Bible* (Chicago: Moody Press, 1986), p. 1667.
9. Ray C. Stedman, *Hebrews* (Downers Grove. IL: InterVarsity Press, 1992), p. 24.

Chapter 6

1. Brigham Young, *Journal of Discourses* (London: Latter-day Saint's Book Depot, 1854-56), 3:93.
2. *Gospel Principles* (Salt Lake City: Church of Jesus Christ of Latter-day Saints, 1986), p. 290.
3. Joseph Fielding Smith, *The Life and Teachings of Jesus and His Apostles* (Salt Lake City: The Church of Jesus Christ of Latter-day Saints, n.d.), p. 327.
4. *Gospel Principles*, p. 17.
5. Bruce McConkie, *Mormon Doctrine* (Salt Lake City: Bookcraft, 1977), p. 601.
6. James Talmage, *The Articles of Faith* (Salt Lake City: The Church of Jesus Christ of Latter-day Saints, 1982), p. 197.
7. Ibid., p. 197.
8. McConkie, *Mormon Doctrine*, p. 24.
9. Ibid., p. 237.

Chapter 7

1. *Doctrine and Covenants* (Salt Lake City: The Church of Jesus Christ of Latter-day Saints, 1990), 93:21.
2. Bruce McConkie, *Mormon Doctrine* (Salt Lake City: Bookcraft, 1977), pp. 546-47.
3. Stephen Robinson and Craig Blomberg, *How Wide the Divide?* (Downers Grove, IL: InterVarsity Press, 1995), p. 16.
4. LeGrand Richards, *A Marvelous Work and a Wonder* (Salt Lake City: Deseret Book Company, 1958), p. 98.
5. James Talmage, *Articles of Faith* (Salt Lake City: The Church of Jesus Christ of Latter-day Saints, 1982), #2.
6. *Gospel Principles* (Salt Lake City: Church of Jesus Christ of Latter-day Saints, 1981), p. 19.
7. *Church News*, 18 March 1989, p. 16.
8. Charles C. Ryrie, *Basic Theology* (Wheaton, IL: Victor Books, 1986), p. 248.
9. Benjamin Warfield, *The Lord of Glory* (Grand Rapids: Baker, 1974), p. 77.

10. I am indebted to Robert Bowman for these evidences.
11. Robinson and Blomberg, *How Wide*, p. 139.
12. David A. Reed and John R. Farkas, *Mormons Answered Verse by Verse* (Grand Rapids: Baker, 1993), p. 53.
13. *Doctrine and Covenants*, 93:21-23.
14. See Robert Reymond, *Jesus, Divine Messiah: The New Testament Witness* (Phillipsburg, NJ: Presbyterian and Reformed, 1990), p. 247.
15. See Geoffrey W. Bromiley, *Theological Dictionary of the New Testament*, abridged in 1 vol. (Grand Rapids: Eerdmans, 1985), p. 968.
16. David Reed, *Jehovah's Witnesses Answered Verse by Verse* (Grand Rapids: Baker, 1992), p. 97.
17. See Marvin R. Vincent, *Word Studies in the New Testament*, vol. 3 (Grand Rapids: Eerdmans, 1975), pp. 469-70.
18. Reed, *Jehovah's Witnesses*, p. 48.

Chapter 8

1. *Gospel Principles* (Salt Lake City: Church of Jesus Christ of Latter-day Saints, 1985), p. 29.
2. Ibid., p. 17.
3. *Holy Bible* (Salt Lake City: Church of Jesus Christ of Latter-day Saints, 1990), p. 697.
4. Spencer W. Kimball; quoted in *Book of Mormon Student Manual* (Salt Lake City: Church of Jesus Christ of Latter-day Saints, 1989), p. 36.
5. *Gospel Principles*, p. 290.
6. *The Bible Knowledge Commentary*, eds. John Walvoord and Roy Zuck (Wheaton, IL: Victor Books, 1989), p. 825.
7. Ibid.

Chapter 9

1. Joseph Fielding Smith, *Answers to Gospel Questions* (Salt Lake City: Deseret, 1958), 2:208.
2. Bruce McConkie, *Mormon Doctrine* (Salt Lake City: Bookcraft, 1977), p. 420.
3. LeGrand Richards, *A Marvelous Work and a Wonder* (Salt Lake City: Deseret, 1978), p. 255.

Chapter 10

1. *Draper's Book of Quotations for the Christian World* (Grand Rapids, Baker, 1992), p. 73.
2. Ibid., p. 65.
3. "More Gathered Gold," electronic media, HyperCard stack.
4. Ibid.
5. Ibid.
6. *Draper's Book*, p. 66.
7. Ibid.
8. "More Gathered Gold."
9. Ibid.

If you run into trouble when witnessing or have any questions, feel free to contact my ministry. We will help you if we can.

Ron Rhodes
Reasoning from the Scriptures Ministries
P.O. Box 2526
Frisco, TX 75034

Phone: 214-618-0912
Email: ronrhodes@earthlink.net
Web: www.ronrhodes.org

Free newsletter available upon request.